The Mood of the World

'It is as though his eyes had no lids.'
Hugo von Hofmannsthal

The Mood of the World

Heinz Bude

Translated by Simon Garnett

polity

First published in German as *Das Gefühl der Welt. Über die Macht von Stimmungen* © Carl Hanser Verlag, Munich, 2016

This English edition © Polity Press, 2018

Polity Press
65 Bridge Street
Cambridge CB2 1UR, UK

Polity Press
101 Station Landing
Suite 300
Medford, MA 02155, USA

ISBN-13: 978-1-5095-1993-4
ISBN-13: 978-1-5095-1994-1 (pb)

A catalogue record for this book is available from the British Library.

Library of Congress Cataloging-in-Publication Data
Names: Bude, Heinz, author.
Title: The mood of the world / Heinz Bude.
Other titles: Gefühl der Welt. English
Description: Cambridge, UK ; Medford, MA : Polity Press, [2018] | Translation of: Gefühl der Welt : über die Macht von Stimmungen. | Includes bibliographical references and index.
Identifiers: LCCN 2018004123 (print) | LCCN 2018020354 (ebook) | ISBN 9781509519972 (Epub) | ISBN 9781509519934 (hardback) | ISBN 9781509519941 (pbk.)
Subjects: LCSH: Mood (Psychology)--Social aspects. | Emotions--Sociological aspects.
Classification: LCC BF521 (ebook) | LCC BF521 .B83 2018 (print) | DDC 155.5/124--dc23LC record available at https://lccn.loc.gov/2018004123

Typeset in 11 on 15 pt Sabon by
Servis Filmsetting Limited, Stockport, Cheshire
Printed and bound in Great Britain by Clays Ltd, St Ives PLC

The publisher has used its best endeavours to ensure that the URLs for external websites referred to in this book are correct and active at the time of going to press. However, the publisher has no responsibility for the websites and can make no guarantee that a site will remain live or that the content is or will remain appropriate.

Every effort has been made to trace all copyright holders, but if any have been inadvertently overlooked the publisher will be pleased to include any necessary credits in any subsequent reprint or edition.

For further information on Polity, visit our website: politybooks.com

Contents

Preface   vi

How We Are, and How We Are Faring   1
In the Mood for 'Mood'   17
Cycles of Contagion and Spirals of Silence   29
Disappointment and Engagement   43
The Relationship Between the Generations   55
The Established and the Outsiders   64
The Feeling of the Sexes   75
The Mood of the Future   87

Notes   95

Preface

Explaining the power of mood confronts sociology with its popular image. The sociological perspective is supposed to reveal ulterior causes and processes: how the popular press manipulates the public mood, the alienating effects of the neoliberal dictate of positivity, how the scandalous facts of increasing social division are suppressed by the feeling that 'there is no alternative'. This book will disappoint any such expectations of sociological explanation.

Mood is not the opium of the people. Moods form a reality of their own and cannot be understood solely as the reaction to biographical circumstances and systemic conditions. While the events of 2008 showed how moods influence events on the financial markets, it has always been assumed that shifts in public mood are responsible for political shifts. It is also abundantly clear just how far our consumer behaviour is dependent on mood. Moods have fundamental significance in a literal sense, in that they convey to us a feeling of the world.

Preface

Depending on my mood, I am capable of anything or nothing. This goes not only for individuals, but also or groups, collectives and societies as a whole. The sociology of mood is thus as fundamental as mood itself. Perhaps more than the sociology of media, the sociology of finance or the sociology of sexuality, it has to do with the social existence which determines our consciousness.

The fifth volume of Karl Ove Knausgård's monumental autobiography *My Struggle* begins with the words:

> The fourteen years I lived in Bergen, from 1988 to 2002, are long gone, no traces of them are left other than as incidents a few people might remember, a flash of recollection here, a flash of recollection there, and of course whatever exists in my own memory of that time. But there is surprisingly little. All that is left of the thousands of days I spent in that small, narrow-streeted, rain-shimmering Vestland town is a few events and lots of sentiments.[1]

How We Are, and How We Are Faring

Have all the melodies of world improvement been played? Does the possibility of the whole appear faint at best? Amidst it all, has the self grown weary of itself? Today, anyone claiming that all truths are relative and that nothing can be trusted is preaching to the converted. Yet the applause is hesitant because many nurture the silent hope that perhaps there is something to believe in after all. That a beginning is possible, despite the complexity of social relations in a world without limits.

Let us not be deceived: the public is watchful and informed enough to know the game of intellectual critique, in which good news about economic growth and job creation is turned into bad news about global warming and the burn-out of the workforce. People don't turn a blind eye to contradictory developments in society and their ambiguous consequences for the individual. Yet intellectual cleverness is considered suspect when it leads to nothing. It appears we have reached the end of a period of perhaps thirty years that many well-known diagnoses of the present see as the grand finale to a longer process of decline. The end of capitalism has again become conceivable;[1] we can imagine a global society that no longer revolves around Europe;[2] and we cast about for metaphors for an Anthropocene[3] that has no equivalent in the millions of years of Earth's history. Yet outrage that the world as we know it has been allowed to self-destruct merely conceals fear about not knowing where to go next.

The mood of our situation can be defined by looking at two complexes. The first is rootless anti-capitalism. It can be found among skilled autoworkers with union membership cards,[4] as well as engineers from R&D departments,[5] among high-performing individualists from Eastern Europe, as well as established conservatives from the West,[6] among 'precariously affluent' single-parent families, as well as two-breadwinner households from the world of high achievers with three or more children.[7] At 'my' workplace, in 'our' family, among 'us' locals the world is in order – but outside, predatory capitalism rages, tearing everything to pieces and holding nothing sacred. We will probably be all right. But how our children will manage, heaven only knows.

Anti-capitalists of all classes and nations see the reason for the ubiquitous 'imperialism of disorganization' in the politically willed and driven transformation of what is now barefaced capitalism. Neoliberalism is the name for a cult of the strong self, one that demands the sacrifice of social community, care for the weak and the collective property of the welfare state. The ideological armies that came to power with Ronald

Reagan, Margaret Thatcher and Deng Xiaoping at the end of the 1970s replaced the 'social market economy' with the 'ownership society'. Only when society served the economy, so the neoliberal credo goes, could the economy serve society. Although they knew the dangers, political majorities worldwide subscribed to this reversal of social relations.

The results are visible today. What is positive about the fact that income inequality in the United States has reverted to levels last seen a century ago?[8] How can it be acceptable that, in a rich country like the United Kingdom, material hardship is increasing despite increasing economic strength? (According to a 2014 study, the proportion of UK households unable to properly heat their homes in winter rose from 14 to 33 per cent in three decades, while national economic performance doubled over the same period.)[9] What explains the fact that, according to a long-term study of wealth and income over the last two centuries, the capital gains of the wealthy few have grown faster than the earned income of entire national economies?[10] Having lost its counterpart after the collapse of socialism, capitalism now lacks all restraints. 'Lunch is for losers' is the motto of the capitalist ideal of relentless competition and wholesale social desolation. The conventions of the good life have been swept away by a regime of total mobilization. Sleep and you risk sleeping through what's new, stay awake and optimize your presence through yoga. All just to turn money into more money.

We saw where this mania of extended and accelerated self-exploitation leads to in 2008. When capitalism finds its apotheosis in a financial industry compliant only with the profit demands of a class of monetary asset holders, then the floodgates are open for the financialization of the world.[11] This rests on the notion that everything that exists and that we attach importance to can be assigned a market value.[12] Money rules the world, not because it is a necessary means of satisfying our needs but because it is the sole and all-encompassing end that justifies all means. No longer are we the owners of labour power that we are obliged to sell to an employer, who rewards us for the passivity with which we submit to his demands. Rather, we have turned ourselves into asset individualists who exploit our own talents and potential for the purpose of total self-commercialization. We thought that, by astute calculations and rational investments, we could take control of our own future; however, we failed to notice that we had become the agents of a 'privatized Keynesianism',[13] covering the risks of others who, relying on us to repay our debts, placed mad bets on an uncertain future.

When the miraculous process of money creation came to a halt, because suddenly the rumour went around that a million or so families in the United States who wanted to live in an area where they could confidently send their children to school could no longer service their mortgages, everyday asset individualists with their savings and pensions had to pay up so that banks 'too big to fail' could offload their toxic assets. In the 2008 crisis and the national debt crises from 2011 onwards, ordinary tax-paying citizens were ultimately held liable for crises that had got out of hand for others.

Whatever form of capitalism they hold responsible, be it turbo-capitalism, predatory capitalism, casino capitalism or finance capitalism, the conclusion of the helpless anti-capitalists is always that humanity has painted itself into a corner. Of course, with our pension funds and building society accounts, we too have become part of the system of self-commercialization that apparently can no longer manage its own risks. All the political class has to say, however, is that there is no alternative. The combined anti-capitalist front of ultra-liberals and residual communists, disillusioned social democrats and muted conservatives, alter-globalists and ethno-nationalists is for democracy and the people but against banks, the media and party politicians.

But who speaks for those who would speak for themselves if only they knew what to say?

The anti-capitalism that sees itself as the 'socialism of capital'[14] cannot be compared to the organized anti-capitalism that defines itself in the confrontation between capital and labour. When the factory was the predominant form of socialization, you knew that the bosses sat upstairs while their stooges kept watch from the windowed offices. However, in the 'factory without walls', where the boundaries between life and work blur, the contradiction between wages and profit, between labour value and capital yields, has been shifted onto the individual. People no longer trust in their own collective strength and instead distrust and demonize the system. The society of distrust feels trapped in a closed system of ubiquitous dependency whose parts are individually animated by selfishness and arbitrariness, rather than somehow combining to produce a rational whole. The terrifying instability of the world elicits a universal indignation triggered by one thing one moment and something else the next. It is the expression of an unease in the world unable to decide whether to reject the world or to affirm it.

The opposite of the outraged anti-capitalists are the relaxed system fatalists. They have long since abandoned the idea of a rational whole with honest merchants, socially responsible entrepreneurs and strong popular parties. They respond to the neurotic anti-capitalists with their hopeless fixation on traditional certainties by pointing to new opportunities, hidden gains and unexpected hybrids. Like it or not, systems are based on the arbitrary will of individuals and the randomness of effects; only these produce the brilliant ideas and daring projects that guarantee the ability of the system as a whole to react to changing circumstances and unpredictable domino effects. Looking back in anger only distorts the view of the future, which you need in order to survive. Overall, relaxed fatalists make a more civilized, versatile and intelligent impression than rootless anti-capitalists, with their suppressed anger, all-consuming hatred and craving for approval.

Relaxed fatalists prefer to sit back and watch than to fret the whole time that things aren't as one might wish. For them, it is more important to survey the field than to improve the world. This allows you to identify your options and be on the ready for the next opportunity. When developments appear to have come to a dead end, then it is simply because of the self-reflexivity of processes with no aim or logic. Because everything could be different, I can change nearly nothing, as the systems theorist Niklas Luhmann put it in the early 1970s in a prescient essay on the risks of truth and the perfection of critique.[15]

In their assessment of the situation, both sides may actually concur: today's younger generation is growing up in a world of uncertain career prospects, increasing income inequality, global political instability and deepening ecological crisis. As the debate on intergenerational equity proves, these facts have become a predominant issue between the generations. The only difference is that fatalists both young and old prefer to scale back their expectations in an attitude of imperturbability, rather than to exhaust themselves through inward or outward resistance.

To make life easier, if nothing else, system fatalists are less pessimistic when it comes to capitalism. It is merely a matter of perspective. After all, 1989 was a hiatus in two senses.[16] The fall of the Berlin Wall marked a historic watershed in the development of worldwide inequality in that, after the collapse of socialist or even communist alternatives caused by economic growth in the newly industrialized countries, the process of divergence between the industrialized countries of the global North and the developing countries of the global South, underway for the past two centuries, went into reverse. The success of China, India, Brazil, Vietnam and South Africa in incorporating and developing the technologies, organizational models and financial practices of the core capitalist nations enabled them to make enormous leaps in growth and to significantly reduce the disparity in living standards between nations. This economic growth steadily diminished the proportion of the poor in the global population. Whether, given population growth as a whole, the relative decrease in global poverty has been sufficient to prevent its increase in absolute terms is an open question. However, one thing is certain: for the first time since the beginning of the Industrial Revolution, economic progress is outpacing population growth.

Simultaneously, however, intra-societal inequalities in living standards, both in the growing economies of the South as well as the once dominant economies of the North, have grown significantly. Everywhere, the social gulf between high earners, median earners and low earners within individual countries has deepened and become more intractable. Things in the world have thus got better and worse at the same time, the system fatalists note wryly. What they don't say, however, is whether they support an attitude of escapism or engagement.

On the overheated property markets of London, Paris and Milan, rich Russians, Indians and Chinese are driving the local middle classes out of the respectable central districts. In Infernetto in Rome, in Neukölln in Berlin or in Bradford in northern England, sub-proletarian survival camps have emerged for people from all over the world; they form a permanent poor population lacking any significant prospects. In the OECD countries, the middle class is splitting into a wealthy upper segment and a precarious lower segment that chafes under the increasing cost of educating its offspring, expensive health insurance – particularly for family members needing care – and rising housing costs in the better locations. In opaque social landscapes like this, it seems prudent, particularly to those not fortunate enough to have inherited or acquired rank, to be cautious, to hold back and to avoid breaking cover, rather than to protest, to stick their necks out and to speak up. In a rapidly changing world, people increasingly wonder whether they feel as at home in society as their parents' and above all their grandparents' generations did during the long post-war era.

Neither the anti-capitalist nor the fatalist position is based on a developed interpretation of the world that one might submit to counter-argument, proof of inconsistency or factual correction. Both are attitudes *towards* the world corresponding to a particular mood *in* the world. The mood is the ground from which the figures of the 'rootless anti-capitalist' and 'relaxed fatalist' stand out. Only in light of this figure–ground relationship is the reason for the relentless antagonism between the two comprehensible. Mood raises the question that prompts the one or other response. It is a question that calls into question how we live and why we live.

Moods are ways of being in the world. A mood of empathy assails us when, on holiday, we drive through a village and come across a funeral procession; a dramatic mood overcomes us during a thunderstorm amidst a landscape; after dreaming about one's childhood, one wakes up in a wistful mood; after a long day, I try to put myself in another mood by listening to a John Coltrane album or a string quartet by Franz Schubert. Just as it is impossible, according to Paul Watzlawick, not to communicate, since silence is also eloquent and ignoring someone is a way of paying attention to them, it is also impossible, according to Martin Heidegger, not to be in this or that mood because contentment is a mood no less than depression, pensiveness a mood no less than exuberance, lassitude a mood no less than agitation.[17]

For Heidegger, mood determines 'how one is, and how one is faring' (*wie einem ist und wird*):[18] how reality becomes accessible to us; what feelings, memories and thoughts suggest themselves and what are excluded from the outset; what kinds of behaviour are deemed appropriate and what are rejected as inappropriate; and, above all, how the world represents itself to us as a whole. However, moods should not be understood as purely private conditions and merely personal feelings. On the contrary, they form the basic tone or general coloration of the understanding and experience of an objectivity that challenges the self to become itself. In mood, the self in a sense becomes aware of itself, and it cannot make excuses for itself through something else that it has nothing to do with.

In Heidegger's deliberately stilted formulation, which on first reading seems impenetrable: 'In having a mood, *Dasein* is always disclosed moodwise as that entity to which it has been delivered over in its Being; and in this way it has been delivered over to the Being which, in existing, it has to be.'[19]

But where does the mood come from that leaves me, when driving past a funeral procession, caught outdoors during a storm, waking up in the morning or listening to music in the evening, feeling this way or that? Mood emerges from the situation I am in, with the impressions, demands and modes of connectivity that it directs at me, and asks me what I understand to be the purpose of my existence and the kind of life I want to lead.

In biographical terms, that may make sense on the basis that a succession of formative moments occurs in the course of one's life,[20] such as starting school, the crisis of puberty and severance from one's parents, the transition from education to work, the decision to enter a permanent relationship or the birth of one's first child. But how can we understand the process whereby mood is determined through a social-historical situation?

Here, Heidegger offers a methodology of 'world disclosure' (*Welterschließung*) that, as Karl Jaspers puts it,[21] asks how the world as a whole discloses itself within time.[22] Do I understand the world in terms of its vulnerability or in terms of its mutability, futility or meagreness? The mood that currently predominates, or that is covertly signalling its arrival, can thus be traced.

Uniting the rootless anti-capitalists and the relaxed system fatalists in their contentious co-dependency is a mood of fundamental tension, one that oscillates between negation of the world and affirmation of it, between escapism and engagement. Just as the anti-capitalists are capable only of pathos, so the fatalists can only do bathos. It is as if the one needs the other as an excuse to start a fight. While the anti-capitalists rage against a politics without alternatives, against 'fake news' and 'dumbing down', the system fatalists celebrate everyday compromise, mass-media self-reference and the relativity of truths. Both positions are so entrenched that dialogue between them about the essence of politics, the production of the public sphere or the meaning of truth seems almost impossible. The certitude of the raging anti-capitalists provokes the arrogant insouciance of the system fatalists – and vice versa: the glass bead game of the serene voyeurs provokes the angry engagement of the world improvers. The one group shuts itself off from the other and withdraws into a bubble of self-semblance.

The general mood of tension underlies the sudden rise of social movements like PEGIDA in Germany and the Tea Party in the United States. Under the banner of anti-politics, distrust and self-empowerment, the worried, the neglected and the aggrieved join forces to voice en masse the constitutive power of the people. 'We are the people!' has been the slogan of all the recent protest movements. Those who feel ignored, downgraded and hard-done-by seek mutual resonance and strength by rising up as a group from a levelled-out middle class.[23]

Publicly, the adherents of refined social observation deplore these campaigns for the restoration of self-respect.[24] As pedagogues of relaxed fatalism, all that they can see in them are the futile exercises of social groups that have not yet understood the lessons of postmodernity. Neither violence nor idealism can change the fact that the age of collective self-determination is past. This unwillingness to accept universal co-dependence in complex systems is seen by the other side as the root condition of grievance, ill will and xenophobia. In terms of its public manifestation, the controversy between rootless anti-capitalism and relaxed fatalism thus becomes the struggle over the minimum of indifference and non-engagement necessary for civilization.

It can't be denied that we find ourselves at the end of a strange period of thirty years, beginning in 1989, during which global social conditions have been getting simultaneously better and worse. For all of us, the world has expanded, opening up new questions of self-realization and new opportunities for self-revelation and re-combination. Unmistakable, at any rate, is the return of the long-ignored Romantic motif of the poeticization of the world, of arrival from the periphery and the reconstruction of disparate fragments.

This underlying mood first reveals itself in a break with the phobic dispositions of the previous era. There is a sense of wanting to free oneself from negative attachments that make one narrow, obstinate and rigid. Just as neoliberalism recoils in panic from anything to do with the state and society, so postmodernity is defined by its fear of the truth.

Thinking about neoliberalism's early days in the late 1970s, what comes to mind is its liberating blow against social sclerosis,[25] against the mentality of vested interests[26] and diagnoses of ungovernability in 'late' capitalism.[27] The 'dream of eternal prosperity'[28] was suddenly shown to be a short-lived and irreversibly defunct ideal, dependent on unique circumstances. However, as the years passed, the energy of mental liberation itself became a structure of intellectual enslavement. Both neoliberals and their critics are driven by a furore trapped in what feels like the automatisms of abhorrence.

Similarly, the postmodernist credo according to which all knowledge and understanding is socially constructed, and hence the ethos of recognizing the manifold ways of knowing and understanding, was originally a huge liberation of the intellect from narrow-minded methodologies and provincial cosmologies. In what at the time felt like a fresh and optimistic mode of thought, postmodernists argued that if we can understand the conventional status of our knowledge and methodologies, then – crucially both for the politics of science and for everyday morality – we will come to see that it is we and not reality who are responsible for what we know.[29]

However, what began as an assertion of openness became in time a doctrine of closure. If the relativity and limitedness of knowledge and understanding are clear from the outset, then what is left to make us want to try to know and to experience the joy at being able to understand? 'Fear of knowledge'[30] came to be an albatross around the necks of a younger generation of researchers, artists, philosophers and intellectuals.

But where are the signs of the emergence of a new mood? One clue can be found in the debate in the visual arts.

Postmodern irony, which once resisted modernist enthusiasm for progress, utopia, functionalism and purism, has lost its appeal here. The combination of nihilism, sarcasm and distrust of grand narratives about the 'irreducible individual' and suchlike has been discarded as stale and empty. One no longer wants merely to endlessly defer the end, to demonstrate the impossibility of narrating the world, to denounce the whole as untrue, but to begin something, to try something, to assemble something. People seek an art of engagement,[31] assembly[32] and vitality.[33] The new claim is: 'Engagement not exhibitionism, hope not melancholy'.

CEOs and politicians, architects and artists alike are formulating anew a narrative of longing structured by and conditioned on a belief ('yes we can', 'change we can believe in') that was long repressed, for a possibility ('a better future') that was long forgotten. Indeed, if, simplistically put, the modern outlook *vis-à-vis* idealism and ideals could be characterized as fanatic and/or naive, and the postmodern mindset as apathetic and/or skeptic, the current generation's attitude – for it is, and very much so, an attitude tied to a generation – can be conceived of as a kind of informed naivety, a pragmatic idealism.[34]

A very different indicator of change in the general mood, this time pertaining to the global situation, can be found in Achille Mbembe's *Critique of Black Reason*, first published in 2013. The book analyses the inherent connection between racism and capitalism, showing how the racial subject was concocted on the plantations of colonialism in the shadow of the bourgeois subject, appearing to the hysterical white ruler as an object that was both threatening and seductive. The term 'negro' was invented as an expression of exclusion, condemnation and humiliation, marking a difference in skin colour that to this day continues to be invoked and detested. Like Frantz Fanon, Mbembe stresses that the colonized person can experience his or her life only as the permanent struggle against a death that is atmospherically ubiquitous. Hence, for the person degraded to a racial subject, the urge for revenge is irresistible, and emancipatory violence is inevitable. The book shows that we continue to live in a racist world where, for the colonized, it is a question of giving meaning not to one's life but to one's death.

Nelson Mandela, who unlike Ruben Um Nyobé, Patrice Lumumba, Amílcar Cabral, Martin Luther King and the rest escaped murder, thought differently. Meditating endlessly in his cell, he arrived at the idea of ontological semblance and proximity between human beings, despite the best efforts of his guards to convince him otherwise. Achille Mbembe comes to a similar conclusion in his epilogue, entitled 'There is only one world'. Given the irreversible intermingling and interweaving of cultures, peoples and nations in this one world, he writes, only a process of reassembling amputated parts, of repairing broken links and of relaunching forms of reciprocity can guarantee progress for humanity and offer a politics for the future.[35]

In the Mood for 'Mood'

For a long time, 'mood' was a rather disreputable concept – and for many it still is. It is associated either with public mood and its manipulation by the mass media, with their lurid headlines and tales of tragedy, or with mind and mood management, yoga and swimming, *muzak* and colour theory, feng shui and ambient lighting, and notions of holism and world harmony. Mood belongs to an entertainment and wellness industry that, in societies like ours, offers respite to the battle-weary soldiers of the wars of competition. Mood's lack of appeal is compounded by the fact that the word's roots are Germanic, and hence not graspable in the Greek and Latinate terms of English scientific and technical language. The word's Germanic etymology also makes it difficult to translate.[1] The problem isn't just one of nuances. Rendering 'mood' as the French word *humeur* captures the emotional constitution of the self, which may be in a good or a bad mood, but this misses the atmospheric reality of a landscape or a group of people, which conveys a sublime or dangerous mood and is separable from the self. In French, this is *atmosphère*. The same distinction is also made in Spanish (*humor*, *atmósfera*) and in Italian (*umore*, *atmosfera*). In German, the word for mood – *Stimmung* – can also mean the 'tuning' of a musical instrument, as well as the specific behaviour of people brought into a feeling of, say, panic or enthusiasm. In its full semantic breadth, the German word *Stimmung* has no exact translation in any other European language.

If these problems are not enough, the concept of mood can also seem like a nebulous compensation for the complexity, disunity and plurality of society. 'Mood', one suspects, is intended to conceal the extent of our own displacement, disillusionment and deracination in the world. Reconciliation that fails to take place in reality is replaced by the mood one brings oneself – or is brought – into. Sorrow immediately alleviated by comfort; pain that takes on cosmic meaning; soul vibrations that send audiences into raptures. Surely mood is kitsch?[2]

This essentially ideological rejection of the concept of mood has for some time been contested since it ignores crucial aspects of human existence. After all, people navigate the world using not just their reason, their categories, their theories and their values but also their feelings, intuitions, emotions and sensibilities. To play one off against the other is to divide human beings' relationship with the world in half.

The modern German concept of *Stimmung* first appeared in the sixteenth century as a musical term referring to the pitch of an instrument. In the eighteenth century, it was used to describe the basic constitution of the soul, and was extended to the relationship between a person and the world. This was the start of an astonishing lexical career that ranged from Johann Georg Sulzer's theory of the dispositions and Wilhelm Wundt's psycho-physical parallelism, to the *Lebensphilosophie* of Fichte and Nietzsche and the metaphysical poetics of Rilke and von Hofmannsthal, and to the existential philosophy of Martin Heidegger and Franz Rosenzweig.[3] The free play of reason and sensibility in the 'balanced temperament' of aesthetic judgement; animation through the unknown forces of the soul; the discovery of an innermost and unique subjectivity; the concentration on stirrings, impressions and evocations in selfless lyrical expression; and, finally, the idea of the self-interpretation of being – throughout the intellectual history of the last two centuries, the concept of mood was constantly defined in new ways. Mood provides a key category for the human being as a whole, which not only structures and analyses the world through the intellect but also rationally comprehends and experiences itself as a part of the world in which it finds itself.

The return of mood as a serious category in the humanities is above all the result of aesthetic debate in literary studies.[4] After the adventures in the 'close reading' of the single, all-revealing sentence, in the 'distant reading' of hundreds of documents in the search for common textual features and in the 're-reading' of anything and everything in the name of the 'linguistic turn', literary criticism has again started looking at emotional and exploratory reading. Now that linguistically sophisticated readings no longer hold out the prospect of revealing anything new, it seems that intuition is back on the agenda.[5] Perhaps what even the purely formal analysis of texts ultimately wants to do is to trace questions that have disappeared into history, leaving only the answers.[6] That, at any rate, is the opinion of Franco Moretti, a critic of the ceremonial and solemn reading of a few select texts, who prefers graphs, maps and diagrams for charting world literature.[7]

One can sense a new mood in the humanities as a whole, a desire to break free from the fixation on language as the beginning and end of human self-understanding. Half a century ago, the shift from consciousness to language meant an intellectual revolution; now the new has grown old.

Exemplary of this trend is the new interest in feelings, whose importance to the thought, will and action of individuals, groups and societies is clearly far greater than notions of 'speaking animals' and 'rational machines' would suggest. When analysing feelings, we cannot exclude the 'lower senses' of smell, taste and touch which, unlike the 'distance senses' of sight and hearing, cannot easily be verbalized. It is possible to recognize someone very clearly from their smell but difficult to say what actually defines it. The haptic distinctions between cashmere and merino, between oak and lime, between sipping tea from a china cup or a stoneware mug, suggest that the spectrum is wide. Wittgenstein's dictum that the limits of my language mean the limits of my world was certainly not the last word on the subject.

Feelings and sensations permit a new view of the

communicative mechanisms of processes of socialization. Taking place beyond the rational coordination of different interests, points of view and preferences are processes of contagion, emulation and adoption, which have more to do with situational encounters than the intentions of actors. The spread of rumours, the dynamics of violence and market fluctuations all give an idea of this.

Finally, there are signs of a need to 'return to the thing itself' (Edmund Husserl). The age of theoretical bias, when what must not be could not be, has left behind the sense that theory distorts our understanding of reality. Human beings are certainly neither the oldest nor the most consistent of problems that human knowledge has posed to itself. On the contrary, after fifty years of self-analysis in the humanities, we know that human beings, with all their idiosyncrasies, differences and similarities, are a fairly recent invention of sixteenth-century European culture. At any rate, it doesn't seem as if knowledge has been acquired or steps taken that might cause the human being as we know it to disappear, like a face drawn in sand at the edge of the sea – as Michel Foucault evoked this supposed moment of parting.[8] In a world where, year on year, advertisers, investment bankers and radiologists converge on the Nevada desert to witness the spiritual spectacle of the 'Burning Man', while youngsters from Bordeaux, Wolfsburg and Liverpool make their way to Syria to fight for ISIS; where millions of micro-decisions are made every second online, and yet where terminally ill patients cannot legally decide the manner of their death;

where big data lets prosumers of the world be minutely categorized on the basis of preference, receptivity and aggregability, while the social gulf within societies between the privileged and the underprivileged grows ever deeper; where social rights have been universalized in some regions, while human rights have been suspended for specific groups in others – in such a world, Foucault's image of the vanishing human being is out of place. More apt would be the 'principle of unfathomability or the open question', defined by Helmuth Plessner as the basis for a phenomenological methodology,[9] thus making the term 'human being' the cipher for the enigma of what we are. Investigating mood can be one way to clarify what eludes us, what lies ahead and what remains entirely obscure.

It seems, then, that as a result of waning methodological certainties, we are increasingly in the mood for a concept of mood. Under such circumstances, there is a growing readiness to face up to things, to collect observations, to gradually gain experience and, step by step, to make generalizations. Freud's remark concerning the empirical method of psychoanalysis is fitting here. 'There is no incongruity,' he said, 'if its most general concepts lack clarity and if its postulates are provisional; it leaves their more precise definition to the result of future work.'[10]

In this mood, what can we say about the metaphorically strong yet semantically vague concept of mood?

As Otto Friedrich Bollnow pointed out,[11] in the German language moods are often identified through the stems *Sinn* (sense) or *Mut* (spirit). *Trübsinn* (gloom), *Frohsinn* (joy) and *Leichtsinn* (carefreeness), or *Übermut* (high spirits), *Wehmut* (melancholy), *Schwermut* (depression), *Gleichmut* (calm) and *Missmut* (ill-temperedness) refer to different kinds of 'being in the mood' that envelop one. If these words are understood literally, the 'sense' of the world correlates with the 'spirit' of the self. This totality of feeling 'comes neither from "outside" nor from "inside", but arises out of Being-in-the-world, as a way of such Being'.[12] Mood is perceived as problematic precisely because it undermines the self-evident scientific distinction between a subject that processes information and an object from which information emanates. The world is present in mood but, instead of being outside me, I find myself within it.

How, then, does a mood overcome me whose essence is neither in me nor in the world, but which expresses the way I am in the world?

Sometimes, one enters a mood seamlessly through 'bodily stirrings',[13] for example in summer on the beach. It is only after three days that one notices one is starting to relax. Sometimes one adjusts to a social situation through the glances, gestures and movements of other people, at a ceremony, perhaps, or at a party or a football match, where there is no escaping the mood. Sometimes, images and stories of unimaginable cataclysms such as war, displacement, inflation and revolution convey the feeling that something is beginning or ending. However, a mood can also take over without there being any apparent cause or social convention that would explain it.

Mood is more than a sum of bodily states; rather,

it dominates me as an overall feeling. Mood endures because of my willingness to feel certain feelings, to expect certain expectations and to predict certain predictions. Worry and bitterness refuse to pass, cheerfulness and contentedness cannot be deterred.

However, I am neither the author of nor witness to my mood. Instead, I understand myself in this mood or that. I cannot escape my own skin, although of course I wonder how long things will go on as they are. This is true of good moods and bad moods, ups and downs. In the former I fear, in the latter I hope that the light will not stay as pallid, soft, cheerful or garish as it is now.

The consequence of this, however, is that the moods that I experience force me to ask myself what it means for me to be in this or that mood. Heidegger plays on this when he says that, in my mood, I am responsible for my being, for what I have to be. In other words, mood doesn't place me in a relationship to the world but in relation to myself. The inward demand that I 'have to be' comes from the fear or the hope that the mood that I am in now will pass and make way for another one. Every mood knows other moods and, as a possibility of being, points to other possibilities of being. The question as to why I exist only arises because self-being as mood is always possible-being as mood.[14] For Heidegger, famously, my certain death is the horizon of this question, which during adolescence, in mid-life or on retirement can suddenly rob me of my sleep in bouts of agitation specific to my stage of life.

Psychology solves the intractable problem of the connection between mood dependence and freedom to be oneself through a conceptual distinction between mood, feeling and affect. In affect I hit back, run away or laugh along with the others. My body takes over and I do what I normally wouldn't. In retrospect, a long film plays before my eyes as if of its own accord. Feelings, on the other hand, are focused on something and allow me to deal with a concrete situation. I feel threatened by loss, exposure or rejection; I am relaxed and contented because of professional success, because my relationship remains sexually intact or after going to the gym in the morning; I am annoyed by the unpleasant remarks of a colleague or the run-down state of the public park. Moods, finally, are directed at nothing in particular. Fear remains, even when there is nothing left to be afraid of; cheerfulness disregards every frown and withstands all adversity; my composure refuses to be shaken even by the harshest criticism and severest of humiliations.

Affects are sudden and short lived, feelings are episodes with intense climaxes, moods last longer. The circumstances that trigger affects are usually obvious. The connection of feelings to specific events emerges through the signals, the explanations and the excuses of the person who has those feelings. With moods, all one has are conjectures about problematic biographical circumstances, failed support networks and irresolvable conflicts. Moods reveal themselves through effects, not causes.

As 'unfocused evaluative states',[15] moods induce particular perceptions of situations. They encourage feelings, memories and thoughts appropriate to a particular mood and prompt a certain posture (for example, a stoop and a slow gait in a mood of dejection; a proud, erect stance and brisk stride in a mood of euphoria). Lastly, they prompt a certain range of behaviours while tending to prevent other, inappropriate forms of behaviour (uninhibited consumption when one is happy and relaxed; frugality when one is annoyed or depressed).[16] This allows one to see and sense another person's mood.

Psychology has also developed ideas about the interaction and reciprocity of moods, feelings and affects.[17] A mood of irritation can turn into a specific feeling of anger at swindlers and freeloaders, which a spectacular tax-evasion case can cause to become an affect of hatred towards classical scapegoats such as 'Jewish speculators' or 'economic migrants from the Middle East'. The role of what Heinz Heckhausen has referred to as 'value bias'[18] in the evaluation of moods is interesting here. Agitated moods are interpreted either positively or negatively, depending on the situation they anticipate ('hope for', 'fear of'). A negative interpretation can trigger feelings of being overlooked and disrespected, which in turn can produce violent affects aimed at the supposedly guilty party.

However, interaction can also go in the opposite direction. Feelings whose occasion no longer exists subside and lose intensity, leaving a mood to simmer. When anger wears off, latent irritability may take its place; an isolated experience of erotic ecstasy may cause a lifelong sense of melancholy at a missed opportunity for love. Of course, moods can also be the result of a gradual accumulation of everyday annoyances or pleasures. Small everyday experiences can combine in a day-long mood of success or failure, when everything seems either to be going well or going badly.

Psychologists have been researching the impact of moods for over a century. From Wilhelm Wundt and the *Gestalt* theory of Max Wertheimer and Wolfgang Metzger[19] to the transactional theory of Richard S. Lazarus[20] and Amos Tversky's and Daniel Kahneman's analysis of mood heuristics, emotional framing and the focusing illusion,[21] there is now a vast literature on the impact of mood on readiness to help others, risk taking, attention span, powers of recollection, attribution tendencies, probability assessment, persuasiveness, cognitive performance, readiness to cooperate, and posture.[22] All these explanations tend to produce models based on interaction, feedback and process, whose advantage is that they dispense with straightforward analysis of causality and no longer posit a connection between cause and effect. Physiological activation also plays a role, as do the five central personality variables of extraversion, neuroticism, tolerance, conscientiousness and openness to new experiences, as well as baseline motivation and, of course, the weather.

Yet psychology fails to understand mood if it clings to the concept of the 'closed human being' who possesses a personal and a private inner world, in which all experience is hermetically sealed.[23] Mood doesn't come into a person extraneously; it isn't possessed and cannot be arbitrarily regulated. Rather, mood exists in the situation that I am in and through which I understand myself. Of course, the position of the sun at a particular time of day comes into it, as does my hormonal balance at any particular phase in my life cycle. What is crucial for mood, however, is how I am affected by a situation that is defined socially, spatially, historically and biographically, one that requires me to participate and play a role. In the mood of the situation, the self-generating self experiences itself as a self that is already generated by the demands, suggestions and syntheses of others. Every space of experienced presence[24] has a mood to which, without much conscious effort, I seamlessly adjust, and which I perceive either consciously by way of social contrast or which I succumb to without inward resistance. It because of this passivity, wrote Jean-Paul Sartre in 1936/7, that the self is able to be affected at all.[25]

Cycles of Contagion and Spirals of Silence

In the nineteenth century, with the acceleration of life in big cities like London, Paris and Berlin, the universal ego of mood became communicative. Collective usages of the concept of mood emerged that are current today: the mood of the stock market, the political mood of a country, the mood of the masses. The communication of mood takes place below the threshold of consciousness, in non-linear, irregular movements. It produces collectives whose magnetism is not bound to established forms of representation and is therefore unstable. Mood can lead to herd behaviour that can be controlled neither extraneously nor from within.

Early sociology concerned itself with how the autonomy of collective mood was to be understood. In 1898 and 1899, the long forgotten but recently rediscovered Gabriel Tarde published two treatises devoted to the topic of the public, the mass and public opinion. In his day, Tarde was the great adversary of Émile Durkheim, whose ideas about collective representation and solidarity Tarde considered a dangerous mystification of the social.[1]

How, Tarde asked, do individuals who live apart from one another in the city or scattered across the country, or far away from one other on the same continent, come to feel that they share the same social world? The answer was: by reading a national or foreign newspaper. The difference between newspapers and books is that the scandalous, terrifying or repellent thing that I'm currently reading about is, at this very moment, being shared by a large number of other people. Each for themselves, they too are reading the same newspaper on the way to work or wherever else. The keen curiosity with which the subscriber, still in his pyjamas, collects the daily newspaper from his letter box in the morning, is accompanied by the unconscious illusion that numerous others are also on their way to their letter boxes. Herein lies the secret of the constitution of a public.

According to Tarde, this feeling of topicality depends not on the pressing facticity of the events, but on the thrilling simultaneity of their cognizance. What is topical is not what has just taken place, but what at the moment is awakening broad interest – even when it is an event that happened long ago. The First World War is suddenly topical again, or a picture of Angela Merkel in her youth. Topical is what is being talked about.

The oddly feverish interest in current events is what underlies the association of a newspaper-reading public, which is subject to suggestion from afar. Journalists are the agitators, authenticity comes from images, truth is claimed through characters in newsprint.

Cycles of Contagion and Spirals of Silence

What Tarde observes is contagion without contact, the transmission of thoughts across random distances and group formation founded on mutual excitements. As Niklas Luhmann said, no one believes everything in the newspaper, but newspaper readers have become used to being second-order observers who decipher everything communicated according to who is communicating it.[2] This means that, as a rule, we read the newspaper whose principles most closely approximate our own assumptions about social morality, so that we can get properly angry at someone else together with someone else. Moreover, we think we know so much about the methods of the mass media that we cannot trust their sources anyway. That doesn't mean that we don't take an interest every morning in what is reported and how it is reported, together with all the other people that form the public. The passion for topicality, as Tarde put it,[3] makes the consumers of mass media sensitive to shifts in the relational messages being communicated along with every piece of information: whether fears of decline are on the rise or, on the contrary, whether obsessions with the past are surfacing; whether commentaries and reports emphasize the mess we're in or whether a desire for change has become tangible; whether journalism means cynical irony or the sincere quest for truth.

The different publics in society form spaces of mood. Maintained by a constant flow of relevant information and mutual excitement, they intensify the experience of society. The social public emerged in the second half of the nineteenth century, along with mass-media technology and the rise of working-class literacy. This brought a democratization of mood, as the spread of literacy throughout society removed the prerogative of the educated classes. It was no longer the colour, smell and light of the garden that, as with Hugo von Hofmannsthal, composed the mood, but rather, as in Alfred Döblin's novel *Berlin Alexanderplatz*, the boom-boom hiss-hiss of the steam piledriver, the collage of posters on the advertising columns and the hustle and bustle of the electric age. The invasion of the boulevard newspaper at the beginning of the twentieth century, which at first was available only from street vendors and not on subscription (hence the term), is evidence that, alongside the elaborated mood code, a more restricted mood code emerged, and that this gradually asserted itself as the central register in the communication of mood. The first boulevard paper sold in Germany, the *BZ am Mittag*, appeared in 1904. The mass media generate a mass public made up of very different social groups. This public wants from its media topicality, emotionality and visuality. The journalistic technique of the 'human touch' caters to this desire by using the face in the crowd to show what could happen to any one of us, and what every one of us longs for. The evolution of the mass media brought the close-up of the human face, the music of existential searching and spiritual negation, and the moving images of everyday lives. With photography, jazz and cinema, the societal communication of mood became a quintessential function of the media; as a configuration of words, images and sound, mood could now reach all social classes equally. The visual aesthetics of Leni Riefenstahl, which inspired the Nike advertisements, the sound of dance-floor king Giorgio Moroder, a Hollywood production like *Avatar*, which shows how artificial figures develop real feelings, or the Marlboro slogan 'Don't be a Maybe' can all be seen as the 'expressive form' of a contemporary mood-complex with global resonance.

Although the inventors of the internet held traditional media in disdain, the principle that anything that is in vogue is news has not been overturned. On the contrary: online news services that deliberately confuse the classical distinction between reporting, advertising and entertainment have only confirmed it. When you need a new headline every three hours to maintain traffic on your website, then the principles of topicality, emotionality and visuality are paramount. The only question is what online media's inherent imperative of acceleration means for the generation of collective moods. A newspaper's journalists give it a consistent idiom that sends out a message. The online provider, however, dispenses with the unique journalistic voice and promotes only the headline or the snapshot, which ideally comes from a 'citizen journalist'. On the web, the contribution with the greatest impact is the one that smears, ridicules, accuses and harms. The model is not the eccentric and digressive gonzo journalism of a Hunter S. Thompson, but the carnival with its titillations, wordplay and slurs. The statistics of 'likes' and 'shares' show what works; whether it is based on the corrupting affects of ridicule and hate is unimportant. The propagandists of online journalism welcome the polarizing effect of such provocations, which they see less as a sign of the extinction of quality journalism than as an intensification of the experience of socialization.

The mood created by online journalism therefore derives less from the content communicated and the relational messages it contains than from the method of direct, affective public address. This suggests a disjunction between an official, serious public, catered to by the traditional media, and an unofficial, popular public that doesn't wait for the interpretations offered by the media but takes the medium into its own hands. Netizens, with their claim to a different kind of sovereignty, constitute a demos opposed to the established representatives of the public interest – to a 'media elite' and 'political elite' that, in the liberal democratic system, presume to speak for the people through the press and parliament, instead of letting the people speak for themselves. It is only logical that this concealed but potent-feeling demos eventually emancipates itself from its origins in the forums of citizens' journalism and instead moves to the blogs and social networks, where it constructs the communicative catacombs of a deep and underlying mood of rebellion. The affects of rebellion – anger and rage – are directed at all those who became immeasurably rich and incredibly corrupt during the 'frivolous years' of neoliberalism. The comedians Beppe Grillo in Italy and Dieudonné in France, both typical spokespersons of this mood, have blogs that are followed by hundreds of thousands of people. They express distrust in the system by reintroducing a vertical divide in political discourse: the divide between the palazzo – the home of the indifferent, slick and cruel bearers of power – and the piazza, where the people are growing restive and angry.[4]

Gabriel Tarde knew that a febrile public can quickly turn into a belligerent mass that marches through the streets and assembles on public squares, chanting its demands and voicing its opinion, extolling something or blaming someone for something. In this sense, the public can be understood as a virtual mass: the public prepares what gets vented by the mass. For Tarde, the transformation of an essentially passive public into an active mass can be extremely dangerous; however, fortunately it occurs only very rarely.

Nevertheless, the transformation is always possible. As Tarde says elsewhere,[5] the public normally leads a quiet life that takes the world for granted. However, random events such as extreme weather, the death of an icon, a single tweet or an image or video shared on Instagram can change things in an instant.

> A mob is a strange phenomenon. It is a gathering of heterogeneous elements, unknown to one another; but as soon as a spark of passion, having flashed out from one of these elements, electrifies this confused mass, there takes place a sort of sudden organization, a spontaneous generation. This incoherence becomes cohesion, this noise becomes a voice, and these thousands of men crowded together soon form but a single animal, a wild beast without a name . . .[6]

Unruly though mass behaviour may appear, for Tarde the mass is not a form of degeneracy. On the contrary, he sees it as an intensification of the social. The mass makes people equal since on the street or the square no one is more important or better than another. The mass channels a diversity of passions in a single direction and towards a common grievance, causing vibrations between individuals based on heightened mutual awareness and diminished self-consciousness. In the mass, the person disintegrates into an assembly of partial objects, which combine and connect with others in their own ways, thereby generating the whole. Shouts combine with shouts, hands with hands, steps with steps. The mass impresses itself with the immensity of its own anger, its grotesque pride, its pathological sensitivity and frightening irresponsibility, thus endowing itself with the illusion of its omnipotence.[7]

On the one hand, then, there is the power of the public, whose mood determines the popularity ratings of politicians, the reputation of a brand or the share value of companies. On the other hand, there is the power of the mass, which as a desiring and demanding, outspoken and potentially violent collective generates the proverbial mood of the street. Finally, both are complemented by the power of public opinion, which is said to predominate within a community and to define the general mood. Motivated by the public, it appears momentarily in the mass, but functions as the 'law of opinion and reputation' like an anonymous censor who, through approval and rejection of suggestions, opinions, conjectures and visions, haunts the spaces of experienced presence. John Locke, who developed the first theory of public opinion at the end of the seventeenth century, during discussions with friends in his London home,[8] explains public opinion in connection with place, in order to clarify that it was a matter of local processes occurring among people belonging to a particular community. He had in mind a civic society of clubs, in which lively discourse was cultivated between parliament, the editorial offices of newspapers, coffee houses and domestic circles. People paid attention to each other, talked among themselves, conversed about events and exchanged opinions. Measured against the views, principles and customs belonging to that particular place, behaviour was either applauded or rejected. At stake for each individual was their good reputation among their fellows.

'Nor is there one of ten thousand,' noted Locke on the basis of his conversations with his friends, 'who is stiff and insensible enough to bear up under the constant dislike and condemnation of his own club.'[9] That means, of course, that the basis of our own opinion is what we presume is the opinion of the other. Every opinion we express anticipates in its very formulation the reaction of the addressee. We do not want to be misunderstood or, if we have a completely different opinion, at least hope that others will be sympathetic. If not, one acquires a reputation for being a 'difficult person', an 'awkward character' or a 'constant moaner'. This led Locke to conclude that what we call our opinion is just a reflection of the opinions of others and doesn't really belong to us.

Two hundred years later, in the mid-nineteenth century, Gabriel Tarde – like Gustave Flaubert in *Madame Bovary* – was thinking more of the French provinces and less of the far-off and urbane capital. In the provinces, debates didn't take place in clubs; instead, conversations of a more or less sophisticated nature were conducted at dinner parties, at the pub or across the garden fence.

In such everyday conversations, the highly personal and the highly general combine quite naturally. We talk about illnesses, neighbours' bad behaviour, quarrels at work and what handymen charge these days; but also about the security of our pensions, the madness of civil wars, conditions in schools and the refugee burden. The tone can alternate between annoyance, despair and relief. Overall, however, the topics, tone and structure of our everyday conversations seem to reflect the situation in which we find ourselves as contemporaries.

There is the anthropological constant of talking about the weather, about aches and pains and other people's incompetence; however, these conversations are repeatedly intersected by the stuff of the moment, as it features in the evening news, the local newspaper or the internet. One gets together, whether seated or standing, to do nothing but talk. Out of this, however, there develops of its own accord 'a chain and an interlacing of questions and answers, or exchanged advice and mutual objections'[10] concerning matters of interest to everyone, or at least what no one can ignore. Facial expression, tone of voice and gesture inform participants about each other's interest in the subject. Mild irony can unintentionally turn into deadly seriousness, or a silly remark trigger a heated argument. This can happen in Japanese reserve, French nonchalance, Italian volubility or German bluntness. These conversations are founded in human sociability, but the mood of the social situation also develops in them. The eclecticism of everyday conversations is what makes them so receptive to the feeling of the world and the thoughts of the age.

The power of mood is thus expressed through its articulation in people's opinions. No one is behind it, pulling the strings. Instead, it emerges through exchange and stabilizes itself through repetition. We return to it automatically, surprised that a feeling of finality, change, inertia has again come over us.

Suddenly, the conversation can take an oddly portentous turn and adopt a national 'master narrative'.[11] A mood of national demise, social division and irreparable loss descends, the reaction to which varies. The American way is to place one's hopes in a charismatic leader who can sweep aside all intellectual misgivings and restore meaning to the nation. The French way is to collectively invoke the Republic, which will turn everyone back into children of the revolution and opponents of globalization. The Germans, meanwhile, appeal to the authority of the law and let regional civil society replace the concept of popular protest. In other words: in Richmond, Virginia, people yearn for a figure who takes the lead and makes America great again; in St Étienne, people vote for a party that despite the schism between the left-wing establishment and the right-wing populists can unite the nation, while at the same time reconfirming the values of the Republic, despite diversity; and in Stuttgart, people express their belief that the law is the law and that the Swabians will never go under.

Yet in the way it communicates itself through

movements within the public, through manifestations of the mass and through the vagaries of public opinion, mood is never unequivocal. Paul F. Lazarsfeld, co-author of the famous 1933 study on the 'Unemployed of Marienthal' and, after emigrating to the United States, pioneer of psephology and opinion polling, explained citizens' preferences through the notion of the hierarchy of stabilities. At the very top of this hierarchy were voting intentions. It is often still the case that the first voting decision of one's life determines how one votes from then on. Generally, it takes a long time before people change their minds, whether on the basis of new options, experiences or developments. At the same time, the mood of the moment often decides election results.

For psephologists, this poses numerous problems. They identify relatively stable preferences, compute them, make a prognosis and on election day get it spectacularly wrong. There are always hangers-on, who at the last minute choose to vote for the probable winner rather than the probable loser.[12] People don't want to be one of the idiots who didn't realize who the majority candidate was. The candidate of the party I prefer, on the basis that it most closely matches my own beliefs about good policy, is not necessarily the one I vote for. Very often, I will opt for the candidate of another party because I think that she is the leader of the majority, and in my social circles I don't want to belong to a distrusted or patronized minority. Better to howl with the wolves than to speak out.

Elisabeth Noelle-Neumann adopted Lazarsfeld's ideas and, drawing on the political philosophy of John

Locke and others, developed the theory of the 'spiral of silence'. This holds that predominant moods result from individuals' fear of isolation.[13] The desire to be on the side of the winner is caused by the fear of rejection and disrespect. I keep quiet about what everyone seems to be saying because I fear being alone with my opinion. Thus a vacillating mood can spread; sometimes, a mood swing may even occur. As a convinced social democrat, I unexpectedly discover positive aspects to the conservative candidate; as a habitual conservative, I am suddenly impressed by the freshness and elan of the social democratic challenger. Mood creates pressure to conform.

For Elisabeth Noelle-Neumann, the public sphere is not a realm of public consultation and mutual recognition, as it is for Jürgen Habermas.[14] Rather, the individual experiences it as a field of threat, somewhere a person can lose face. I exercise restraint, note what others say and, if in doubt, follow the lead of the opinion formers. For Noelle-Neumann, people are fearful and cautious by nature. To think otherwise would be unrealistic.

Whatever one thinks of this sceptical anthropology, it is supported by the sociological diagnosis that, as Norbert Elias put it, we live in a 'society of individuals'.[15] Depending on the strength of their attachment to large-scale collective categories such as class or citizenship, and the extent to which advertising, entertainment and journalism address the public in national or merely local terms, individuals become the playthings of stimuli, seductions and amusements. The self experiences itself as an affective being dependent upon reinforcements and exposed to mood. When it feels alone, the self is scared and silent; when it believes that many others think and feel as it does, it thrives and meets approval. Whether in retirement or in public, the self is determined by mood. All that matters is its assessment of the mood of the majority – whether the self, together with all those who hold their tongues, vanishes into a spiral of silence; or whether, in unison with those willing to talk and be seen, it masters the mood.

Disappointment and Engagement

It would certainly be wrong to see the 1950s solely as an era of personal advancement, withdrawal into the private and social conformity, the 1960s solely as a decade of political passion, sexual liberation and general non-conformity, or the 1970s solely as an era of self-realization, egoism and lawlessness. This would be to overlook the futuristic World Expo in Brussels in 1958, featuring André Waterkeyn's 'Atomium', which represented the elementary cell of the ice crystal enlarged 165 million times over, and Le Corbusier's electronic poem, composed with Edgar Varese and Iannis Xenakis. It would be to overlook that the 1970s saw the rise of the 'new social movements' for peace, women's rights and the environment, together with new social status for the respective milieus. The story sounds more simplistic still when you concede that, while it may apply to the OECD countries, the situation was very different in Vietnam, where the Americans were waging war, or in South Africa, which was under apartheid rule, or in Iran, which was suffering under the Shah regime.

Yet it can't be denied that the shift from Frank Sinatra to Elvis Presley, and from the Rolling Stones and the Beatles to ABBA and the Bee Gees, marked a change of mood. When Frank Sinatra – dressed in casual suit and holding a heavy whisky glass – sings 'In the Wee Small Hours of the Morning' in 1955, he is invoking the dark side of a strong desire for security and comfort. When Elvis, dressed in black prison denims, gyrates to 'Jailhouse Rock' in 1957, then the floodgates have been opened to 'sex, drugs and rock 'n' roll'. 'A Hard Day's Night' by the Beatles in 1964 and 'Satisfaction' by the Rolling Stones in 1965 strike a completely different register of excitement than 'Money, Money, Money' by ABBA in 1976, and 'Stayin' Alive' by the Bee Gees in 1977, from the film *Saturday Night Fever* starring the young disco phenomenon John Travolta. Here, a shift reveals itself from the pathos of liberation to the art of survival: a confession of the impossible ('I can't get no') is replaced by an assertion of perseverance ('stayin' alive').

Economic historians place this development in the context of the post-war boom and the recession in the 1970s;[1] analysts of political culture emphasize the shift from the materialist values of duty and conformity to the post-materialist values of self-realization and individual development, and then to an unclear synthesis of both;[2] sociologists of the family look at how practices of socialization went from being authoritarian to permissive.[3] However, none of these perspectives is able to grasp changes in people's emotional experience of their lives, which are based on mood change. How, then, is collective mood change to be understood?

A highly instructive model for understanding collective mood swings was provided by Albert Hirschman in the 1980s.[4] Interestingly, Hirschman was neither a sociologist nor a psychologist, but a political economist. Hirschman found the key to explaining moods through studying experiences of disappointment. Moods, he argued, become collective via a history of shared disappointments or, more precisely, disappointments in relation to one of the central aspects of modern human experience: consumption.

We all know what it's like to spend lots of money on a smart car, an elegant chair, a new-generation tablet or some other expensive item, only to have doubts about its usefulness soon afterwards. The tablet's ID isn't as easy to set up as the manufacturer says; the narrow chair looks elegant when other people sit in it, but you yourself find it uncomfortable; and when you drive around in your SUV, it isn't looks of respect that you garner but derisive remarks about its exorbitant fuel consumption and senior citizen-friendly seat height. Did I make up my mind too quickly? Did I consider the costs of maintenance, cleaning and system compatibility thoroughly enough? Isn't all this status-related consumerism not terribly irritating and strenuous?

Consumption must be learned, above all when it comes to durable commodities whose mere presence confronts us incessantly with the possibility of having made the wrong choice. When ideological disappointment about the 'cultural meaning' of the product – as Max Weber would say – is added to the mix, then consumption stops being pleasurable and becomes a torment.

The manifold forms of consumer asceticism, from veganism to car sharing to fair-trade guarantees, can be interpreted as signs of habitual uncertainty about real enjoyment and its conspicuous display. This explains the astonishing anger that consumer ascetics have towards consumer virtuosos. Instead of seeking inner peace, they are mainly concerned with the behaviour of others – people whose meat consumption causes animals to be tortured and killed; people who, because of their style of consumption, squander valuable resources, hasten global warming and endanger the survival of the species.

For Hirschman, consumption was the most important sphere in which groups and individuals participate in modern, complex and highly diversified society. Through our opportunity and capacity to consume, we demonstrate our sociability and get the feeling we belong to the party. Without consumer means or consumer skills, we soon feel excluded from society as a whole.

It is natural, then, that upwardly mobile groups are particularly enthusiastic consumers, celebrating their rise with new forms of consumption. The mobile phone cult among young people with migrant backgrounds or the passion for German cars among social climbers generally can be seen as evidence of this. At the same time, however, they are particularly susceptible to disappointments when their expectations completely fail to be met. This usually happens with second-generation migrants, whose education makes them particularly sensitive to false promises. Electronic gadgets and convertibles are then no longer enough. They want exclusive hotels for the romantic holiday and top-of-the-range Dutch prams. Of course, when mixing with the upper class, swimming with the tide often means having to swim against the tide. Conspicuous consumption becomes a source of nagging doubt and recurring uncertainty.

According to Hirschman, in the late 1950s and early 1960s, a sense of disappointment spread en masse amongst the upwardly mobile groups of the post-war era. The 1961 novel *Revolutionary Road* by Richard Yates tells the story of a perfect young couple living a suburban existence in Connecticut, USA, in the mid-1950s.[5] Like a post-war Madame Bovary, April is trying to make it as an amateur actress; Frank, who was conscripted at eighteen and is just old enough to have taken part in the spring offensive against the Germans, has a well-paid job selling office machinery in Manhattan. Living in a single-family house in the 'Revolutionary Hill Settlement', with their two children, French windows, lawn mower and electric cooker, they soon lapse into states of mutual silence lasting days. Seeking escape from the 'desperate loneliness' of life in the post-war boom, the couple talk about moving to Paris, where Juliette Greco sings 'L'Éternel féminin' in the basement bar Tabou, and Simone Signoret and Yves Montand live out a very different kind of relationship. Away from the sterile neighbourhood idyll, from the dire advertisements for the revolutionary concept of computer-aided data processing, from the grinning void of the television and from their acute feelings of guilt and endless self-reproach about their wasted lives. Above all, away from the optimistic, permanently jocular, breezy sentimentality that everyone views life with. Neither clinging to one another for dear life nor the illicit adventure of sexual infidelity can prevent this young couple, during the post-romantic phase of their relationship, from feeling trapped. At the beginning of the 1960s, this parable of personal failure amidst an exploding world of commodities expresses the yearning for an existence beyond the truncated ideals of private happiness and personal advancement.

Hirschman points out that consumers' silent experiences of disappointment require public articulation before one can feel what one feels. In 1960, the 31-year-old German writer Hans Magnus Enzensberger published an article in *Die Zeit* entitled 'The Plebiscite of the Consumer'. In it, West Germany's long-awaited 'angry young man'[6] analysed the autumn catalogue of the mail-order company Neckermann, describing the 'petty-bourgeois hell' of a consumerism without alternative. Customers could choose between IRISETTE and OPTILON, SUPREMA and KINGFLASH, TURBOFLEX and DANUFLOR, MINICARE and ERBAPRACTIC, SKAI and LAVAFIX, NO IRON FINISH and NINO-IRIX-AUTO-MAGIC. Moreover, this mumbo jumbo was presented in an insidious mix of moronic sentimentality ('our dear customers') and catchy progressivism ('mainframe computer'). Enzensberger anticipated how his critique would be answered. These are the concerns of arrogant intellectuals who only wish to deny ordinary people's pleasure at being able to participate through consumption. Objections of this kind, however, do nothing to diminish the sureness of his verdict on the disappointments of consumerism:

Never before have the German proletariat and the German petty-bourgeoisie lived in a state so close to idiocy than today, in 1960. Is it snobbery to note this dangerous fact with a cry of regret? It is by no means our intention to defend Mr N., the publisher of the catalogue we have before us. His company's willingness to please is the sort that would do whatever was demanded of it. However, no one will be able to blame Mr N. alone for what, with such diligence, he registers and exploits: a social failure for which all are to blame. Our government, for whom the stultification of the majority appears convenient; our industry, which is grateful for the thriving business; our trade unions, which do nothing about a mental exploitation inconceivable during the material impoverishment of the past; and our intelligentsia, which wrote off the victims of this exploitation long ago.[7]

There must be a pause to allow a mood change to take place. All at once, stability loses its charm and change becomes appealing. Hirschman speaks of a repulsion effect where one wants to get rid of something that has become boring and painful. With the student movement of 1966–1968, a mood of political passion suddenly spread across Western European societies and some Eastern European societies too. The withdrawal into the private sphere stopped being seen as a reasonable reaction to world war and genocide and began to be

condemned as an evasion of questions of social responsibility and a diminution of human possibilities. A new
generation raised its voice, condemning the absence of
any concept of public happiness and instead searching
for emotive formulas for political engagement. In Paris
and Prague, Berlin and Berkeley, Tokyo and Caracas,
Amsterdam and Seoul, students took to the streets, as
the saying goes, to herald the mood of a new era.

Hirschman was not interested in momentary moods
that decide elections. Instead, he wanted to understand
epochal mood swings that intersect the histories of
national societies and define historical periods. Willy
Brandt, in his inaugural speech as German chancellor on
28 October 1969, famously declared, in accord with the
general mood across the western world:

> We want to dare more democracy. We will reveal how we
> work and want to satisfy the critical need for information.
> We will give every citizen the opportunity to participate
> in reforming the state and society, and not only through
> hearings in the Bundestag, but also through our constant
> contact with representative groups within the population
> and by offering transparency about government policies.[8]

The word used by Brandt for this new form of 'contact'
with the population is the strange term *Fühlungsnahme*
(literally 'testing of feelings'), thus making clear that
mood is the currency of politics.

We know today how quickly this mood evaporated.
Brandt, who achieved the biggest electoral victory
in the long history of the Social Democratic Party of
Germany, resigned in May 1974. The 1970s went on to

be dominated by politicians who raised no hopes for the future: Jimmy Carter in the United States, who in July 1979 made his depressing 'malaise speech', criticizing the materialism and consumerism of his countrymen and reminding them of the limits of growth; Leonid Brezhnev in the Soviet Union, who could do nothing to prevent the increasing obsolescence and paralysis of socialism; Zhou Enlai in China, who turned the final phase of the cultural revolution primarily against artists and journalists; and Helmut Schmidt in Germany, whose car-free Sundays lent his crisis-management style a distinctly ascetic character and who, as a veteran of the Second World War, accepted the Red Army Faction's domestic 'declaration of war'. The left-wing terrorism of the Red Brigades in Italy, the Japanese Red Army, the Weathermen in the United States, the Tupamaros in Uruguay and the Red Army Faction in West Germany[9] are evidence of the huge disappointment at the perceived failure of political engagement in complex societies, which for the socially critical and engaged wing of the student movement turned out to be a system of inconceivable expansion and elastic boundaries. It seemed simply impossible to do anything about the falsehood of the world (or 'the bullshit around us', as Jefferson Airplane put it).[10]

The arrival of punk at the end of the decade – after the beatniks and the hippies – marked the third and perhaps last distinctive sub-culture of pop, after the beatniks and the hippies. With their slogan 'No future!' – intended as a positive assertion – they consistently refused social-critical interpretation as a way of improving the general capacity to live meaningfully. The mood of the punks was an aggressive affirmation of the present without obligation to the past or responsibility for the future. After the Sex Pistols' band member Sid Vicious stabbed his girlfriend Nancy Spungen in the Chelsea Hotel in New York on 12 October 1978, Vivienne Westwood, the 'Queen of Punk', made a T-shirt emblazoned with the words 'She is dead I'm alive . . .' in red smears on white jersey.

According to Hirschman, collective moods come in two basic forms. Central to the first is the endangered self, which seeks to secure its narrow life-world against the incursions of strangers, the demands of society and the claims of the state. The aim is to get ahead, to make use of the opportunities that arise and to lead a peaceful and respectable life both individually and as a family. Things requiring long-term investments are valued highly: building or buying one's own home, educating one's children or a hobby like collecting stamps, first editions, vinyl or football paraphernalia. The people that run society are expected to stabilize the conditions for running one's life and to ensure a certain degree of law and order.

It is conceivable that such a mood emerges after periods of exaggerated collective spirit, false promises and exploited enthusiasm. Experience has shown that a politics of excessive engagement can destroy everything. It seems more civilized, cleverer and more humane to reject abstract principles, to withdraw into small units and to get on with one's life.

The second mood is sustained by the feeling that

there must be more to life than the pursuit of personal interest. The world is regarded as space of opportunity with few givens and much that can be done. A sense of unease prevails that contains both the fear and the hope of another way of being. All you have to do is open your closed self to the other. In a state of 'sweet delirium', as Pier Paolo Pasolini put it in a poem called 'Dunckler Enthusiasmo' of 1950,[11] you will see that, together with others, you can move mountains. This mood of participation, of discussion and collaboration, is founded on an experience of synchronicity with others with whom all you share is the urge to move forward in unison, to leave behind the silence, the repression and the suspicion. You guess perhaps that you will end up alone, but crossing boundaries seems more interesting than drawing them.

Because nothing can be held onto forever and because all that one has devoted so much to becomes stale, it is worth taking a step into the unknown, not just mentally, and not alone, but together with all the others who want more than just to survive. The heightened sense of the present, which is what is at stake in this mood, is more important than accustoming oneself to and accommodating oneself in a protracted moment where the present never passes.

The experience of the 'negative' freedom to refuse to be spoken for, to be overpowered and threatened strengthens the yearning for a 'positive' freedom that consists in being willing to commit oneself and, collectively, to start something new. Contrary to the mood that nothing remains to be done except to process the debris of failed projects, one prefers the feeling that one is living on the cutting edge.

The negative in Hirschman's model is the expectation of disappointment – among the enthused and disillusioned alike. The positive is trust in the cycle – that every withdrawal into privacy and security will necessarily be followed by a movement towards openness and publicity.

Nevertheless, trust in the cycle assumes that new groups will continue to emerge who, full of energy and confidence, demand a share of the commons. Mood swing depends on upward mobility and demographic change. Suddenly, voices make themselves heard that had not been on the radar. Their group identity is based on professional success, educational aspiration, the will to influence and consumer clout. When people stop daring to seize power and claim entitlement, mood swings come to a halt. Change in consumption is an expression of social mobility. According to the political economist Albert Hirschman, when demand runs out for commodities that improve life and whose purchase is worth the effort, there can be neither disappointment nor engagement.

The Relationship
Between the Generations

Today, it is 'Generation Y' that is making waves. 'Y' stands for 'Why?', in other words for a generation that asks about the whys and wherefores. Or it may simply refer to the generation after 'Generation X', meaning those born between the end of the 1960s and the beginning of the 1980s, who were the first to make the acquaintance of McJobs and accept precariousness as a life prospect.[1] Between the Generation X of the 1990s and the Generation Y of the 2010s, the world has changed fundamentally. It has been a long time since a generation was courted as eagerly as today's cohort of university graduates and first-jobbers in their mid- to late twenties. The reason for this is the glaring discrepancy between the birth rate and the number of vacancies. In Germany, the rate of employment has been increasing for some time, reaching around 43 million in 2017, the highest point since reunification. Despite widespread predictions about general deregulation, permanent full-time employment is rising, more older people are in work and the number of attractive jobs in the knowledge-based and specialized service-sector industries is increasing. The problem is that there are fewer people of employment age. Germany's Federal Employment Agency calculates that, if the rate of employment remains constant and if immigration is not factored in, the available workforce will fall from its current number of 45 million to 32.5 million in 2025, a loss of around 6.5 million.[2] There is a shortage of manpower for skilled labour, professional service-sector employment and highly qualified research and development positions. Under such circumstances, every halfway qualified and apparently suitable person counts. At least in Germany.

Ten years ago, a senior consultant conducting interviews for the position of a junior physician would have been able to invite a small handful of the best candidates from a pile of applications, and then have been able to grill each one about why they were qualified for the job. Now, the same consultant has to put up with two young women and a young man asking her what training opportunities and funding programmes the hospital can offer. And if she doesn't show some flexibility on the question of night shifts and overtime, she finds herself after the interviews left without a definite commitment.

'Work–life balance' is at the top of the agenda for these young people. The job must offer interesting challenges that allow them to develop, the hierarchy must be flat so that teamwork can thrive, working hours must be flexible so that the compatibility of work and family is more than just wishful thinking, and the boss must regard herself as a coach who injects the team with the necessary spirit. In a word: 'We won't let ourselves become slaves at work, but if we are convinced by something, then we'll give it our all.'[3]

For the first, post-war generation to emerge from the rubble, the motto was 'live in order to work'. For the generation that grew up during the economic miracle, it was 'work in order to live'. For the ascendant Generation Y, work and life are no longer dissociable. For them, it goes without saying that they can live while they work and work while they live.[4] This means being respected in the workplace but also that their employer understands that the job doesn't mean everything to them, and that the principle of individual support that they are used to from school continues in their professional lives.

Not surprisingly, this generation is given the VIP treatment by a thriving generational research sector.[5] They are stylized as 'secret revolutionaries' who, with creative pragmatism, digital know-how, parental support and ego-tactics learned at an early age, are rupturing the relationship between the generations. Not by complaining, dropping out or rebelling but, ever so softly, by cultivating and asserting a style of enhanced self-efficacy. Unspectacularly, they are changing the world through the silent performance of a 'psycho-economy'[6] of improvisation and flexibility, whose flipside is disillusionment and indifference. Eulogies to them contain a note of wariness, lest these twenty-somethings succeed in pulling the wool over one's eyes: 'In their inconspicuous way, they are subverting traditions that seemed eternal, subtly evading what was supposed to be inevitable, quietly annulling laws society considered irrevocable.'[7]

No wonder, then, that this attitude is not universally loved. In any organization, be it a hospital, a mid-sized auto-parts supplier or a publishing house, different generations of employees converge. The management level still includes members of the post-war generation born in the mid-1950s, whose parents lived through the war and genocide, and whose elder siblings believed in peace and love. Then come the baby boomers born between 1956 and 1965, the trainers-wearing managers and middle-managers who reached adulthood during the oil crisis, punk and the Berlin Wall, who have either come out on top or have been passed over in the permanent competition for positions. They are followed by Generation X, today's forty-somethings who discovered hedonism and MTV in the 'roaring nineties' (Joseph Stiglitz) and who saw their chance in the 'creative destruction' of capitalism, but who frequently backed the wrong horse. And then come the Ys, who can score points as 'digital natives' and who attempt the biographical balancing act of living, learning, working, loving and caring.

The mood of the moment is negotiated between these generational mood-tendencies. This negotiation takes place between the three types famously identified by Karl Mannheim: a leading, a diverted, and a suppressed type of generation.[8] Who is in charge and who is the bearer of hope, whose attitude to life no longer fits and who can still find a mooring, who can change course elegantly, despite their opinions and experiences?

Not surprisingly, there is little love lost between

The Relationship Between the Generations

Generation X, with its painful experience of life's randomness, and Generation Y, which adapted to life's randomness from the outset. It makes a big difference to your mood if you end up where you never wanted to be – or, when making decisions about jobs, commitments and life, you keep your options open, so as to turn accident into opportunity. Many 40-year-olds today think they know what's at stake. Many 20-year-olds saw school and higher education as nothing more than a game that, at the risk of being thought a swot, you could only win through cunning and calculation. Generation Y thinks Generation Xers are whingers, while Generation X thinks Generation Y is arrogant and bratty.

A baby-boomer couple born in 1964 lacks the energy even to worry about the concerns of a first-jobber born in 1984. They are completely preoccupied with helping their oldest child revise for A-level maths and keeping the younger one away from the binge drinkers. At work, they are about to make their final step up the career ladder, while married life has also seen better days. They both find it annoying to have to deal with this new generation, whose brazen demands basically capitalize on their demographic advantage. The baby boomers find it hard to take the Ys seriously – while the Ys think the baby boomers are hopeless workaholics, except for perhaps their parents and their friends.

Of all the generations, those born around 1954 are without a doubt the most politically influential. Angela Merkel and many others in leadership circles in Europe were born in 1954. Now in their early sixties, they have entered the celebrity phase of their careers. The first generation to follow the heroes of 1968, they are characterized by a watchful, reserved and measured style. They don't boast about their life experience but lead by example, drawing attention to things and pointing out omissions. They come from an intermediate position of after and before: after the '68ers, whom they observed close up during the formative phase of the '68ers' biographies as teachers in schools and universities; and before the onslaught of the baby boomers, who were fed up with the 'limits of growth' and embraced the carefree and unencumbered 1980s. As the rearguard of the '68ers, they are reflective and affirmative, and as the vanguard of the baby boomers, they are still marked by the feeling that everything can go wrong.

Being sandwiched like this prompts the '54 generation to read more closely, to question more precisely and to judge more impartially. Helping them to do so were 'joyful thinkers' like Michel Foucault, Gilles Deleuze and Paul Feyerabend. These gave them a sense of how revolutions often rest on illusions, but also of how the status quo can lead astray. In both insights, they are the children of the post-war era: in their anthropological scepticism towards political enthusiasm; and their insurmountable awareness of the 'total collapse'.

Today, the prevalent mood between the generations is determined by the adoption of Generation Y by the '54 generation. Bridging the biographical gap of around thirty years is a similar style of reticence, fear of over-identification, and a pragmatic approach to problem solving. Too much heat and everything burns. They prefer to let things happen rather than commit too quickly to things that end up slowing them down. The more options you have, the fewer the restrictions.

They accept the uncertainty of the world. The risks that individuals are expected to bear are balanced by the protections which one is entitled to from society. Neither generation sees a contradiction between individual responsibility and public support. The same goes for the supposed antithesis between private and public ownership. Not everyone needs their own car, but that doesn't rule out owning one's own home. Both generations expose themselves on social media to test how far self-perception and others' perceptions of them need reconciling, however only to better protect the personal proprium of the self. Connecting the last post-war generation with the first generation of neoliberalism is the mood of a life lived in compromise.

A silent game of mutual transferences lends this relationship, which excludes the intermediate generations, a peculiarly intimate mood. The elders recognize their image in the younger generation, seeing a reflection of their own fears and longings: above all, the fear of ending up alone, expressed through the 'life technique'[9] of non-commitment and the habit of distancing themselves from everything that is too demanding and too challenging, of avoiding embarrassment come what may. The fear of failing at something in particular, at a certain point, become the fear of having done everything wrong. Then, obsession with self-optimization merely camouflages existential crisis.[10] The '54ers view the '84ers as a difficult generation, but also as a generation in difficulty.[11]

The younger generation, who recognize in the older

generation their own life technique, develop an aversion to repeating the established pattern. Their annoyance at having to endorse the pragmatism of the older generation can turn into a search for a lifestyle that is not just pragmatic.

For the generations that have been excluded, this intergenerational symbiosis of mood is somewhat suspect. The baby-boomers born around 1960 don't care too much and merely hope that these post-war melancholics will soon hand over the reins. Using state-of-the-art management techniques with special emphasis on staff diversity, they hope that they will then be able to motivate Generation Y to work harder and identify with the job more. However, the 40-year-olds of Generation X can barely conceal their jealousy of this generational 'pairing', as it is referred to in Wilfred R. Bion's psychoanalytical group-therapy.[12] They see it as an emotional coalition based on a false stabilization, one that refuses to acknowledge what else is happening in the world. For example, in Silicon Valley, a fierce race is under way to develop the 'disruptive' technologies of an industrial revolution that is proceeding exponentially, digitally and combinatorially. Much of what Germany, with its export-driven high-productivity economy, manufactures in the way of machine tools and industrial plants will soon be able to be made more cheaply, more quickly and more precisely elsewhere.[13] Engineers and entrepreneurs in the newly industrialized countries are waiting eagerly to supply the global market with all sorts of new products. In Europe, meanwhile, an intergenerational dream-team is musing about a brave new world of equal opportunities, paternity leave, same-sex marriage and tax breaks for families.

Karl Mannheim offers reassurance from the distant past, together with some fundamental insights. In his lecture held at the Sociology Congress in Zurich in 1928, entitled 'Competition as a cultural phenomenon', he pointed out that:

> There are periods in modern history during which a representative generation becomes free to achieve a synthesis. Such generations take a fresh approach in that they are able to envisage from the higher platform of a synthesis those alternatives and antagonisms which their fathers had interpreted in a dogmatic, absolute sense. Then, if there are existential problems not yet ripe for a solution, such a generation will experience them in entirely different contexts; the old antagonisms, however, become less sharp, and it will be possible to find a point, so to speak, farther back, from which partisan positions can be seen as merely partial and relative, and thus transcended.[14]

The Established and
the Outsiders

So far, talk has been of agitated public spheres, upwardly mobile groups and intergenerational relations, as if we were dealing with ethnically neutral or uniform collectives. Of course, in societies like ours, this is something we can no longer assume. We have long ago outgrown the ethnically homogenous milieu famously described by Joseph Schumpeter.[1] With the exception of the distinctly xenophobic Japan, all the economically developed societies of the OECD are immigration societies in one way or another. There is no doubt that a classical immigration society like the United States has a different foundation to Great Britain, which still sees itself as the core nation of the Commonwealth, or to republican France, where French citizenship replaces all other affiliations, or to Germany, the 'delayed nation' that long resisted seeing itself as a country of immigration. There is no country that has not been affected by the great exodus in global society.

In each case, however, the key factor in determining

social mood is how locals and immigrants – whether new or settled – get along. With migrants and refugees, a distinction is immediately made between country of origin and country of destination, between natives and newcomers, between locals and foreigners – and between 'the established' and 'the outsiders'. Why some people feel entitled to tell others what to do, while others find themselves being told, and what this form of interdependency means for the national mood, is not so easy to understand as one might think.

Norbert Elias, the great theorist of the civilizing process, addressed this question in a seminal study on processes of power formation in an urban settlement, published in 1965 as *The Established and the Outsiders*. In 1960, together with John L. Scotson, who had worked as a teacher in the town, he had looked closely at social life in a typical English working-class community.[2] Their research revealed a deep divide between a group of older residents and a group of newcomers, each of which lived in clearly distinct districts: the established residents here, the outsiders there. Elias and Scotson were interested in how a power balance emerged in which one side could feel powerful and the other side powerless. Contact with 'them over there' was avoided; scare stories were told about broken families, bad-mannered children and irresponsible parents, while people belonging to the anti-social group were denied entry to social circles like the church, clubs and the local council. In general, members of the established group saw themselves as pillars of the community, the cohesion of which was threatened by a lack of communal spirit on the part of the outsiders. Everyday gossip about the thriftlessness, promiscuity and hostility of the people on the other side of town played a central role in preserving the asymmetry between 'good' and 'bad' members of the local community. Bad behaviour on one's own part was passed off as an exception; however, when the others behaved similarly, this was seen as typical of them. The sociologists observed that the newcomers adopted an attitude of bemused resignation and appeared to accept that here they counted as belonging to an inferior, less respectable and not particularly robust group. Even when commenting ironically about how mad the locals were, the subordinate group were clearly extremely vulnerable to attack.

How did the established come to act as if they were better, socially superior and more responsible, and to brand the outsiders as vulgar, spiteful and dissolute? In this case, the usual explanations for power imbalances – class, nationality, ethnic origin, religion and education – were of little use. Both groups belonged to the English working class and some even worked at the same company in similar positions. All that distinguished them was how long they had lived there. In other words: the established based their sense of power, entitlement and rank solely on the knowledge that they had got there first, and that they therefore had the right to demand that the others, the newcomers, fall into line. First come, first served. Whoever arrives later joins the back of the queue and waits their turn.

The law of social time is what, in the minds of the established, entitles them to treat the newcomers like outsiders, to condemn them as irresponsible, anti-social and uncivilized. Outsiders may be given the right to develop, however only according to the standards dictated by the established.

The established thereby indirectly admit that the outsiders can gradually reclaim the power of agency and collectively turn the tables on otherness. The accusation of civilizational deficiency begins to be countered by the accusation of narrow-minded arrogance, so that a stalemate in the power balance comes to seem possible. However, as long as the power gap between the two groups exists, the inferior group's vilification of its counterpart, be it darkly satirical or deadly serious, remains essentially harmless. When it does start hitting its mark, then this is a sign that power is shifting from the rigidified establishment to the flexible outsiders.

At the beginning, however, is the simple claim to have been the first to arrive on a particular territory and thus to be superior to those who arrived later. While this claim can be backed by economic, military or political power, the power of the established is primarily and predominantly based on their will not to let their control over a space be contested by the presence of intruders.

The established therefore often observe the outsiders with a mood of supercilious apprehension, resentful intentness and stubborn inflexibility. There is no humour, no tolerance, no generosity. And what is the mood of the outsiders? The migrants avoid the locals, try to avoid talking about sensitive issues and, when they meet their compatriots in the square outside the station or in the café with the satellite TV, they dream of returning home. As long as the culture of the insiders holds no appeal, abandoning this hope would be too painful. Their hard labour in the foreign country is only tolerable with a suitcase under the bed. At best, locals and migrants live next door to one another: 'How's it going?' asks the friendly student. 'Could be worse,' replies the migrant worker with a smile of resignation and reserve.

Günter Wallraff's *Lowest of the Low*, published in 1985, changed things. Describing the life of temporary worker Ali, it forced the established public to admit that its mood of more or less friendly indifference was no longer tenable. Having placed an advertisement reading 'Foreigner, strong, seeks work of any kind, including heavy and dirty jobs, even for little money',[3] Wallraff had entered the hell of agency work disguised as a Turk named Ali. Taking undercover journalism to its extreme, the book opened up a new perspective on the 'established–outsider figuration'. Business reacted (working conditions for industrial cleaners markedly improved), politics reacted (the minister for employment made reforms a personal priority) and the unions, after initial hesitation, also reacted to what remains the bestselling work of non-fiction in post-war Germany.[4] Its iconic cover shows the author complete with black moustache and a hard hat bearing the Thyssen logo; in the background is an industrial waste ground and, on the horizon, rooftops and trees. After that, migrants were treated as members of society and not just as a workforce.

In 1974, a decade before Wallraff's book, the singer Udo Jürgens released the song 'Greek Wine', together with an album of the same name. The lyrics signalled a shift from indifference to empathy:

It was dark as I walked through the suburban streets. / Light from a bar was shining onto the pavement. / I had time and was cold, so I stepped inside. / Sitting there were men with brown eyes and black hair / And out of the jukebox came music that was strange and southern. / When they saw me, one stood up and offered me a drink. / Greek wine is like the blood of the earth. / Come, have a glass, / and when I get sad, / it's because I'm always dreaming of home; / please forgive me.'

The guest detaches himself from the group of guests, buys the lonely host a drink, and explains why he, the guest, is so awfully sad.

A year after the publication of Wallraff's bestseller, the author Aysel Özakin, who today writes only in English but who then wrote in German and Turkish too, criticized Wallraff's use of the objectivizing and instrumentalizing term 'Turk'. 'Are we all repressed and naive?' she asked. The postulated 'we' of the established was now opposed to the postulated 'we' of the outsiders.

Özakin based her argument on what today would be called 'identity politics'. 'I'm on the verge of losing my confidence and self-respect here in West Germany,' she wrote. 'Partly to blame is a well-meaning, humanist German progressive who wants to protect me (i.e. Ali) as a member of a minority and turn me (i.e. Ali) into an object of sympathy.'[5] The mood of inclusion on the part of the established elicits a mood of resistance on the part of the outsider.

This shows how the power balance between locals and migrants shifts across generations, according to what extent the children and grandchildren of migrants claim their entitlement to respect and consideration in the recipient society. The articulation of rights now happens through the marking of difference. My individual particularity is connected to my conceptual otherness – and it is as such a complex person that I want to be honoured and respected.

That is why the headscarf can raise the question of individual identity. Muslim women claim a collective identity in order to emphasize their individuality. For outsiders, as with Aysel Özakin, confidence and self-respect can only be gained through the public declaration of group belonging. The 'I' attaches itself to a 'we' in order to become an 'I'. For migrants, denying their own migration history is not an option; on the contrary, the question for them is how to capitalize on it.

Characterizing the history of the relationship between the established and the outsiders is from now on the search for a narrative for the new power balance: what do the established concede to outsiders and vice versa?

As long as the established treat the outsiders exclusively pedagogically, helping and supporting them to learn and catch up, nothing changes; equally, nothing changes as long as the outsiders annoy the established by demanding more and more while expecting less and less. All that happens is that a mood of mutual apathy and misunderstanding takes over.

A classic and highly instructive narrative for the new constellation is that of the lions and the foxes. The lions dominate the field, upholding the rules and guarding the entrances; the foxes move around inside the field, bending the rules and trying to get their foot in the door. The foxes have the 'combative residues', the lions take care of the 'group persistence'.[6] If necessary, the lions maintain law and order by force, while the cunning foxes are always in motion and causing a disturbance.

Members of the established group who regard themselves as lions understand that, without movement, deathly silence descends and, for that reason, they respect the foxes; outsiders who act like foxes respect the lions since, without orderly parameters, there can be no opportunities to exploit. The two don't necessarily get on, but if they are honest they will admit that they depend on each other.

In this sense, the tense relationship between migrants and locals always entails competition between energetic status-seekers and defensive status-preservers.[7] This seems less problematic during periods of collective upward mobility, when the escalator is on the way up, than in periods when some are getting more and more while others are getting less and less. Increasing income divergence and the emergence over the last twenty years of detached milieus locked into low social status[8] harms the mood between migrants and locals in two ways. Among the locals, there are groups who feel threatened by the migrant foxes, who they see are doing well in business, catching up in education and competing sexually. For migrants, the distinction between the winners and losers of migration becomes increasingly apparent. Hoping that education and a cosmopolitan milieu will improve their children's chance of social advancement and bring them higher status, the migrant middle classes are fleeing urban areas full of aimless youths and religious fundamentalist rebels. Across Europe, the civilized migrant lions are distancing themselves from the feral migrant foxes. The former want to go their own way, peaceably and cordially, while the others dream of ostentatious lifestyles and glorify the 'community of descent'.

The question of who arrived first, so crucial in the distinction between the established and the outsiders, also plays a major role between migrant generations. Particularly between new and older migrants, it is immediately established who is at the top of migrant society and who occupies the second row. This underlies the 'ethno-racism' among migrant groups. In the playground, it can turn into violence between youngsters of different ethnic backgrounds; however, it is above all relevant when it comes to the regulation of public-funded programmes and the granting of entitlements, where different migrant interest groups compete for the same 'pots' of money.

This was certainly the situation in Germany in the first half of the 1990s, when hundreds of thousands of ethnic Germans from the former Soviet Union, along with refugees from the civil wars in Yugoslavia, came streaming into the country. 'Russian Germans', 'Turkish Germans', 'Vietnamese Germans' and asylum-seeking refugees entered into mundane negotiations over who among the successive waves of migration was entitled to what benefits, pension payments and degrees of public attention. In this new playing field, who are the locals and who the newcomers?

Today, the question poses itself in connection with the refugees that have come to Germany in apparently incalculable numbers and who, when the borders were opened in late summer 2015 during the first idealistic phase of reception, were greeted with open arms by 'biological Germans' in Munich, Hamburg and Stuttgart. What did this gesture of hospitality towards migrants from Syria, Afghanistan, Albania and Ethiopia mean for the Turkish, Greek and Italian migrants who had been living in Germany for generations? Had the conventional hierarchies of place been suspended, or was this just a brief episode of euphoria within a longer and more difficult process of reconciliation?

Above all, how do eastern Germans in eastern Germany feel about the events? Compared to established western Germans, easterners still see themselves as outsiders. Although they may have joined the Federal Republic formally, for them reunification has not meant being placed on an equal footing with the rest of Germany. The fact that the current German chancellor is from the east seems not to alter this impression. For many in eastern Germany, Angela Merkel has stopped being a representative and has become the agent of a foreign power. One swallow does not a summer make.[9] It was the others, the inhabitants of mid-sized towns across West Germany, who got there first and who are still the ones responsible for the success of Germany's high-productivity export economy. It is only when western Germans go to eastern Germany as professors, managers and theatre directors that they are seen as outsiders. Then it is they who, if they ruffle feathers, run up against the rules of the insiders. The first will never be last. If we try to understand the migration process in terms of the 'established–outsider figuration', then we inevitably encounter feelings of shame, envy, revenge and fear. All of this feeds into the mood of the moment.

The Feeling of the Sexes

When, in Jean-Luc Godard's 1963 film *Contempt*, Brigitte Bardot tells Michel Piccoli to his face: 'I hate you because you don't move me' – this comes after scenes in which the woman and the man take the game of seduction to its limit, where they talk endlessly about their love, where they come to blows in desperation, where they pledge their unconditional love – then this articulates a sense of the impossibility of an encounter between the sexes in ways that may say more about the historical moment of desire than birth rates, women's employment rates or rates of divorce. In other words, in order to understand what was driving men and women, or people with other sexual identities, at any given moment, the biopolitical statistics need to be seen in the context of the mood between the sexes. What attracted them to one another, how did they relate, what did they expect from one another? The feeling of the world is always the feeling of the sexes.

Why else do we look at fashion photography – at

the street pictures and portraits of Will McBride from the early 1960s, or of Richard Avedon from the early 1980s and Jürgen Teller from the early 2000s? Because we want to know how erotic differences were displayed, how lust concealed itself, what betrayed the loneliness of lovers. How many shirt buttons did men leave undone? How proudly did women show their legs, cover their bosoms and emphasize their backsides? How brutally did youth revel in itself? If men stop wearing hats (and start wearing caps) and if women stop wearing dresses (and start wearing trouser suits), then the times have changed. Even the transgender code, which abandons the heteronormativity of binary sexual signs in favour of a sophisticated unisex casual look, is discerning about material, looseness of waist, concealment under the hood, all of which create an erotic element. The mood of society is documented in the fashion of the sexes.

It is women who are responsible for shifting the balance. There are still highly educated, confident and professionally successful women who, anticipating the long road of motherhood ahead, choose to break off their careers and leave the role of breadwinner to the man alone. However, they are making a personal biographical choice among many possible lifestyles rather than bowing to the pressure of a gender role that offers them no alternative. The arrangement between the sexes, in which it is mainly the man who brings home the money for the family, posing as the normative authority for the basic unit of society while effectively leaving it to the woman to take responsibility for running family life and doing the housework – this division of familial labour belongs to the past. The vast majority of couples want domestic equality, regardless of their level of education. Both ideally want jobs and a career, while at the same time having a happy family life where the men are active fathers and the women are responsible for more than just cooking and child rearing. Anyone, man or woman, who holds the opinion that a woman's place is in the home needs to have strong backing in a corresponding ideological milieu. Whoever agrees with (or without) Simone de Beauvoir that men equal transcendence, and that their role belongs outside the home, where they earn the money, while women represent immanence and are responsible for making the home comfortable, providing emotional support and looking after the children, does so knowing they are in the minority. After the Second World War, male dominance in societies like ours forfeited its hypnotic power, as Virginia Woolf put it.[1] The mythical boundaries between the sexes, which once made gender roles so rigid, have collapsed.

This is another way of saying that women have been the primary beneficiaries of the education expansion and are now valued on labour markets as employees with high reserves of human capital. Replacing the young woman from a conservative, rural working-class household as the benchmark for a compensatory education policy is the urban male youth from a migrant family with no history of advanced education. Not only do more girls take A levels than they did, they also outperform boys and do better at university. It won't be long before they break through the glass ceiling of graduate studies, at least in the subjects they prefer. This applies even more to ambitious young women with migration backgrounds.

However, it isn't just better preconditions for female careers that are putting women ahead. Changes in self-perception are also crucial. For young women today, it goes without saying that a happy life includes both a good job and a family. They don't want to compromise on either of these two goals. Women who have prioritized their careers over children are seen as negative examples. Despite the overwhelming evidence of a persistent gender pay gap in the labour markets, women's employment rate continues to rise. In some branches, particularly the corporate service sector and professions like medicine, law and psychotherapy, women will soon overtake men, even if their income remains average.

In a thought-provoking book, the American author Hanna Rosin anticipates the 'end of men and the rise of women'.[2] She refers to the situation in 2008, when the politically induced collapse of Lehman Brothers left many family men without a job, unable to repay their mortgages and facing ruin. Germany experienced something similar in the final stages of the Second World War, during the aerial bombardment and the mass exodus of refugees from the eastern territories. In this hour of extreme need, women came to the rescue.[3] Faced with the complete failure of their men, amidst social collapse and under deeply adverse conditions, the 'weaker sex' revealed its strength, putting on a show of incredible resilience and adaptability.

Hanna Rosin infers from this that, in the future, women will take the lead in globalized societies.

Because of their educational advantage and emotional reserves, they are far better equipped than men to deal with 'normal catastrophes',[4] difficult circumstances and uncertain situations. Soft skills like team-play ability, collaborative talent and a subtlety become evolutionary advantages in an economy marked by rapid change, deep social divisions and extended interconnectivity. Methods of power have become more fluid, mobile and ramified, promoting women who make decisions as 'female' but acting as 'male'.

What does this irrevocable shift in the balance between the sexes mean for the mood of society?

There is no denying that men's loss of effortless privilege, the result of the vigorous rise of opportunities for women, has affected the relationship between the sexes at the deepest and most private levels. However, the dynamic of social equality has not been simultaneous with a change in erotic tension, in the sexual script and in the feeling of being desirable, attractive and in demand, whatever one's sexual orientation. A woman in a senior position with three well-adjusted children can suffer because her husband has forgotten how to seduce her in bed. On the other hand, a man with only moderate professional success and personal sophistication, but who still enjoys 'a bit of nookie', may find he is enjoying more popularity with the opposite sex.

The rituals of eroticism often originate in a different era than the rules of sexual equality. Of course, one shouldn't confuse things: a wink across the desk can quickly become sexual harassment and an invitation to dinner an attempt at bribery. However, the two levels can't be separated entirely. The relationship between the sexes, at work and in public, always entails tension which is reflected in the erotic musicality of social relations. That is why the frisson between Ingrid Bergman and Humphrey Bogart, in Michael Curtiz's *Casablanca* of 1942, reflects the wartime mood of the forties; why the love affair between the youthful Mariel Hemingway and the middle-aged charmer Woody Allen in Allen's *Manhattan* of 1979 captures something of the downbeat mood of the seventies; and why the romance between the ageing couple Diane Keaton and Jack Nicholson in Nancy Meyers's *Something's Gotta Give* of 2003 conveys a sense of passing time typical of the 2000s.

Sexologists are unanimous that the modernization of sexual mores and sexual self-perception has given rise to a negotiational or consensual morality[5] that allows for mixes of freedom and civility, desire and courtesy, transgressive self-gratification and acute awareness of boundaries. One feels confident to do what one likes, while at the same time making sure that the other consents to one's preferences or fantasies. Everything is possible, so long as you stick to the rules of taboo-free negotiation and mutual consent. It is not institutions like the church or the state that determine sexual mores, but sexual partners themselves. Regardless whether you are religious, consider yourself a loyal citizen or even hold public office – everyone has sex in their own way and won't let anybody tell them otherwise. You need not have a BDSM fetish; you can also live a chaste married life or get your sexual fulfilment from the missionary position – the main thing is autonomy and mutual respect.

This communicative sexual morality can be understood as the result of two discursive shifts in attitudes towards sex. First, the 'sexual revolution' of the 1960s and 1970s, which in communes, holiday resorts and self-awareness groups brought a fundamental liberalization of sexual desire. Slogans like 'make love not war', controversies over clitoral and vaginal orgasm, or theories about sexual frigidity and petit-bourgeois narrow-mindedness opened up a new way of thinking about the truths of sex. This was followed, however, by the free-choice discourse of the 1980s, which placed limits of civility on the deregulated sexual marketplace. Feminists, 'safe house' activists and men writing about 'male fantasies' took the innocence out of sex. It was revealed how the aristocracy of manhood formed itself through constant, silent and imperceptible commands intended to make women and other non-men willing to accept arbitrary prescriptions and prohibitions as natural, obvious and self-evident.[6] Perhaps the most important development of all, in view of AIDS and its many victims, was the debate about the methods of responsible sexual autonomy. Since then, sexual freedom has meant being liberated, relaxed and curious, but always with mutual feedback and without hierarchies and coercion. In other words: safe, sane and consensual. For cultural critical post-'68ers like Michel Houellebecq, whose bleak satire takes aim at the rebel generation and its illusions of emancipation, the modernization of sex ends in the puritan, demystified and dreary mood of 'social democratic sexuality'.

At the same time, this open-minded, consensual-negotiational morality disrupts the automaticity of sexual interaction for its protagonists.[7] The claim that 'she was asking for it', invoked afterwards by a disrespectful masculinity, is no longer tenable. The ethos of negotiation demands particular sensitivity towards boundaries drawn both verbally and non-verbally. Women and men are empowered to decide and define at every stage in the erotic sequence; to signal stop and go to the other. A kiss is just a kiss, a passionate embrace is merely the expression of physical attraction, an invitation to come upstairs for coffee is really just an invitation to a cup of coffee, or at least not necessarily more than that. The collapse of the conventional automatisms of sexual interaction supposedly gives women more freedom for erotic initiative and sexual assertiveness and enables men to try out a more relaxed and passive interpretation of the gender role imposed on them. Neo-sexualities can emerge that cannot immediately be labelled feminine or masculine. Sex propagates itself, engenders hybrids and transgresses boundaries.

But what does this new ethos of erotic-sexual negotiation look like in reality? Has the mood between the sexes become more relaxed or more strained, calmer or tenser, more liberated or more hung up?

Instructive here is a study of couples which, in so far as the man is no longer the breadwinner, can be seen as absolutely modern.[8] One couple belongs to a milieu where individual fulfilment is the highest good.

The woman provides for the relationship as a well-paid business consultant, the man pursues his vocation as a poorly paid translator. They agree that they need enough for a halfway comfortable life but that money is by no means all that matters. The woman doesn't mind maintaining her partner and the man doesn't find it odd to be maintained. They defend their unconventional lifestyle, to which both contribute. The woman admires the man for his independence and single-mindedness but can't deny that she would like to see a bit more professional ambition. Despite being unhappy with his small income, the man doesn't dispute this. Beyond this silent quarrel, however, there has not yet been a serious conflict between the two.

The problem is that their feelings refuse to play along: the woman admits to being plagued by the traditional need to be taken out to a nice restaurant and be desired and seduced as a woman. The man finds this conventional and leaves her alone with the problem. Sex turns out to be the sore spot in the relationship. More could be going on, the woman thinks. One could attempt to reassure them that after a certain point in a steady relationship, usually between four and seven years, sexual desire fades. However, the partners refuse to settle for this commonplace. The more the woman wants to be desired, the less the man wants to desire her. It is the man's lack of sexual interest and not the woman's that increasingly becomes a problem for the relationship.

This case is proof of the paradoxical relationship between social equality and erotic disappointment. The reversal of social roles cannot allow a re-reversal of erotic roles. Otherwise, everything would be perfect: thanks to the woman, the man could escape the strain of professional rivalries and dedicate himself to his true interests, while continuing to play the role of seducer and phallic conqueror. The woman could surrender herself sexually to the man and no longer be confined to her role as breadwinner. This cannot happen, however, since the man would feel that the woman had triumphed over him completely. Both partners end up withdrawing into the shells of their selves, celebrating the phantom normality of the emancipated couple, as Erving Goffman might have put it.[9]

Does this explain the game of auto-erotic hide-and-seek that so many partners play? That is to say, the preference for masturbation over mutual gratification. It would also account for the extra-erotic dissipation of masculinity in extreme sports, and the notable irritability of professionally successful women of around forty with big handbags and extra-large cups of coffee.

But let's not delude ourselves: things look even worse outside relationships. Today, around 95 per cent of all sexual contact takes place between long-term partners. Singles make up 25 per cent of the population but get only 5 per cent of sexual contact.[10] Life as a single is clearly pretty frustrating sexually.

After looking at different types of relationship, which vary greatly according to social milieu, the authors of the study arrive at a more diagnostically open formulation:

It seems that the more uncertain female and male identities become in modern life, the more significance is placed on the sphere of eroticism and sexuality as an outlet for 'forbidden' yearnings for archaic roles and traditional forms of femininity and masculinity. It seems to be the only area where gender, i.e. the radical difference between man and woman, can be pleasurably performed and ritually expressed.[11]

This interpretation corresponds with sexologists' observation of a need for a new performance of gender difference.[12] There is now discussion of the difference between the privileges of social gender and the representation and performance of cultural gender through outfit, gesture and attitude. Difference encourages exhibitionism in public, in photos or as online avatars. Gender distinctions offer a vast cultural register for the creation of surfaces intended for the gaze of others. I want to create an effect with my sexuality, make myself attractive through my difference, exhibit myself in various ways. It should also be added, however, that the talent for such performative pleasure is not equally distributed between the sexes.

Reporting on an audition marathon with aspiring actors at a regional theatre, a journalist for the *Frankfurter Allgemeine Zeitung* makes the following observations:

These women don't want to be beautiful, dreamy or even emotional. None of Chekov's sisters are on stage here, at most a Viola swearing in Swiss dialect. And yet these young women play their vulgarity with wonderful grace; they yet again celebrate the end of male dominance with such pleasure that it is a delight to watch. And the men? They breathe heavily. In contrast to their female colleagues, whose acting appears effortless, whose rage and hysteria seem to come so easily, they need lots of accessories, lots of external help, to create an effect. They wrap themselves in black leather jackets, bite on blood capsules and fling themselves onto the stage with torn shirts and soaking hair, screaming and whispering, stamping and wailing. And taking care that their freshly shaven armpits don't get dirty. They are sensitive and metro and want so dearly to come across as proletarian-archaic.[13]

The Mood of the Future

In his famous 'postscript', Gilles Deleuze described our society as a society of self-control.[1] Families are centred on children, who are supported along their life's path by attentive, empathetic and encouraging parents. Schools subscribe to the principle of individual support and treat learning as an independent process with teachers acting as companions. Universities offer the full breadth of knowledge while leaving aside the question of truth. Companies are enterprises with open-plan offices, flexitime and flat hierarchies. Hospital treatment is geared towards short stays and self-healing. Formerly, one had to start each phase of life anew, graduating further only after the successful completion of various 'developmental tasks'. Today, in the age of pleasurable creativity, lifelong learning and eternal play, we are never finished with our lives. The limited freedoms of the past, whether during youth, at the weekend or on holiday, are replaced by permanent deferral. To travel hopefully is better than to arrive.

The ubiquitous mood of self-motivation, self-monitoring and self-realization essentially has only two possible releases: acceleration or contemplation, self-optimization or self-absorption, intensification or escape.

The mythical place of acceleration is Silicon Valley. It is detached from the rest of the country, which appears to be undergoing an inexorable process of decline: on the one hand, there is the world of the privileged, with organic supermarkets, cooperative book shops and schools for creative learning; on the other hand, the world of the underprivileged, people who subsist on bad food, cheap education and gruelling multi-jobs.[2] In Silicon Valley, work is underway to create a society of global digital platforms that provide not just everything that can be transformed into information, but also everything that can be extracted from information. Ethnologists who have studied the world's most powerful valley[3] tell of a tribal territory where all that matters are personal recommendations, permanent networking and visible presence. It is here that electronic payment systems get invented for immigrants without bank accounts, data glasses that allow you to recognize other people's emotions, or apps for dating people in your area on the basis of just a photo. Only in the community of the tribe can this kind of thing be developed. Tribal elder Peter Thiel, the founder of PayPal, explains: 'The biggest risk with start-ups is inventing something that already exists or not thinking it down to the final detail. You can only combat this risk with openness during the development stage. Whoever makes a secret out of their project has lost.'[4]

The idea is to design a world where the permanently self-controlled self is wrapped in a perfect info-sphere.[5] Individuals can update themselves about their own consumer preferences, movement profiles and patterns of affinity in order to anticipate what they would have done anyway. For the providers of such a future, of course, this offers huge opportunities. Giving consumers what they want is no longer enough; now you need to know what they will want when they get to middle age or when they reach the peak of their talents. This goes not just for the private economy of commodities but also for public services and state welfare departments. In the age of global data-trading, market, state and civil society merge.

However, the accelerators of Silicon Valley go further still. The digital fusion of biotechnology, pharmaceutics, robotics and nanotechnology raises the possibility of an irrevocable transformation of the species. Ray Kurzweil, founder of the Singularity University in Silicon Valley, which is financed by Google, genuinely wants to develop a machine for everything that has been thought in the past and that will be thought in the future. This will complete the digital evolutionary process of Google.[6] First comes navigational optimization through the search engine, memory supplementation through management software for emails and pictures, and reality enhancement through imaginative glasses and lenses. The next phase is artificial intelligence and the self-educating machine and brain amelioration through the implantation of digital amplifiers. Finally, to crown it all, a cloud will emerge that will store all methods of human knowledge and be equivalent to total consciousness and pure mind. All we have to do is sever the associative mechanism of the mind from the neurones and transfer them to transistors.

It is no longer the knee or the thumb that is the most human part of the human being but the concealed, mysterious brain. This brain-centredness reveals just how radical the extreme accelerators are.[7] By perfecting the closed circuit of control in which the self confines itself, they are trying to escape it. The way out of the system is the way through it.[8] As Brecht said, one should start not from the good old things but the bad new ones. The result, however, is a mood of absolute intellectualization that combines enthusiasm for the new with relaxation towards the absolute. Surpassing the world becomes the condition for transforming it. What is left is the mundane, physical and mortal part of the self, the zero of existence that is the beginning of everything.

The other form of release is to retreat into an otherworldly place where one can avoid accelerated self-control. It feels as though one has passed the threshold from ordinary, agitated existence into extraordinary, peaceful existence. The counterpart of Silicon Valley would be something like the cloistral practices of deceleration offering silence, transcendence and simplicity. The society of control can only be escaped by abandoning self-control and allowing oneself to be controlled from afar. This transcendental referent usually has a religious connotation, but one that appears neither authoritarian nor conventional.

The various methods of deceleration usually emphasize exercises and rituals over arguments and beliefs. Like with the weekly yoga class, you can participate freely without bothering with the theories of some guru or other. Far from being suspended, the mundane, physical, finite part of the self becomes the point at which deceleration techniques begin.

Just as in Silicon Valley, deceleration involves initiation into an exclusive community. Smartphones are left outside. The community isn't tied to a particular place but can form everywhere and anywhere, so long as you stick to the prescribed rituals. Meditation offers a break from the digital everyday and allows you to concentrate fully on the here and now. Be silent, feel the others and resonate with the universe.

Yet this inner composure usually means absolute self-closure. You block out the world with all its tensions and are alone with yourself. Just as the machines of communication, contact and control cannot reach you, nor can anything else. Withdrawal from the self often accompanies indifference to others. The self can only rescue itself from its own self-control by rejecting the world. Real experience, the goal, is not the mental reduction of the multiplicity of things but the existential reduction of desires and consciousness as such. The goal is to find inner peace through the mystical completion of the ego.[9] Such moods idealize the phlegmatic states of contentedness, calm, composure and reflection, rather than the choleric, sanguine and melancholy states.[10]

But what about the generations of the future, those who don't get carried away by fantasies of total power or seek escape in egocentric mysticism? They are people who, timidly, reservedly and shyly,[11] see a different beginning. They want to leave behind an era of agitation and indifference. They are conservative in a fundamental sense, in that they see no sense in a disintegrating world where all that matters is security for yourself and your kin. It is a world that has given up on producing futures offering liveable lives to people beyond one's narrow circle.

Of course, they also don't want to cling to things that serve only to fend off a menacing future. Unnecessary battles waste energy and tend to stem from a troubled psyche incapable of satisfaction. Their progressivism is therefore based on insight and not desire.

The future generation dissociates itself from previous generations, which it believes have got caught up in ironic self-delusions that merely amplify a sense of sad weariness. For all their pretences, these want nothing better than to lie down and sleep. Though capable of cruel lucidity, previous generations all too often subscribe to weak thoughts that, confronted with irrefutable reality, fail to bear scrutiny. The future generation distances itself from a mood of dejection and apathy that condemns all visions as ideologies and predicts defeat before anything has even begun. They much prefer the generation before, the 'angry old men' who with slogans like *indignez-vous!* (Stéphane Hessel) or 'Reinvent the future' (Michel Serres) have also dropped their inhibitions. The future generations are not the bleating lambs of a barbaric capitalism, but nor are they the obnoxious puppets of the digital era.

With judicious scepticism and watchful reserve, the future generation seeks new openings in a world of diminishing space and elapsing time. There is no place on the planet left untouched where one might build a new world. In the Anthropocene, humans alter nature; in the 'second machine age', machines alter humans; and in the 'info-sphere', the mind alters the body. The future has always already begun, which is why hoping for a new age is no longer possible. In every generation, something disappears and something appears; even the difference between past and future time becomes meaningless. The future generation is prudent and takes on responsibility, but it doesn't believe in moralizations like 'intergenerational justice' or 'sustainability', which contain far too much teleological piety. Blaming the wasteful lifestyles of older generations for diminishing younger generations' chances in life is all too obviously an existential evasion. As if humankind could change what happened all over the world long ago.

The future generation accepts the world, limited as it is, as the sphere of its beliefs, feelings and actions. Hence the pragmatic ethos of experiment that is motivating top graduates of elite US universities to venture into unknown territory rather than go to Silicon Valley. They want to dare to start anew, to feel resonance with others, to intentionally scale down. Their motto is a full life with a minimum of principles. Grand intentions that fail to bring self-efficacy are held in contempt just as much as settling for a false life and giving up on the idea of authenticity. Ethical know-how[12] has something to do with communal immersion, personal courage and social engagement. No one wants to belong to a 'bunch of nobodies'[13] who go through life behaving like stage directors, actors and spectators but who have no sense of being partners or participants. Openness to the world without self-negation: that is the mood of the future.

Notes

Preface

1 Karl Ove Knausgaard (2016), *Some Rain Must Fall: My Struggle Book 5*, trans. Don Bartlett, London: Vintage.

How We Are, and How We Are Faring

1 Wolfgang Streeck (2015), 'Wie wird der Kapitalismus enden?', *Blätter für deutsche und internationale Politik* 60(3): 99–111.

2 Dipesh Chakrabarty (2000), *Provincializing Europe: Postcolonial Thought and Historical Difference*, Princeton.

3 Paul J. Crutzen (2002), 'Geology of Mankind', *Nature* 415 (3 January): 23.

4 Klaus Dörre, Hajo Holst and Ingo Matuschek, 'Zwischen Firmenbewusstsein und Wachstumskritik. Empirische Befunde aus einem Industriebetrieb', WSI-Mitteilungen 67(7), *Grenzen des Wachstums – Grenzen des Kapitalismus?*: 543–50.

5 Stine Marg, Lars Geiges, Felix Butzlaff and Franz Walter (eds) (2013), *Die neue Macht der Bürger. Was motiviert die Protestbewegungen?*, Reinbek bei Hamburg, p. 48ff.

6 Gero Neugebauer (2006), *Politische Milieus in Deutschland. Die Studie der Friedrich-Ebert-Stiftung*, Bonn.

7 Hans Bertram and Carolin Deuflhard (2014), *Die überforderte Generation. Arbeit und Familie in der Wissensgesellschaft*, Opladen/Berlin/Toronto.

8 Thomas Piketty and Emmanuel Saez (2003), 'Income Inequality in the United States, 1913–1998', *Quarterly Journal of Economics* 118(1): 1–39.

9 Heinz Bude (2015), 'Brennpunkte sozialer Spaltung', in Steffen Mau and Nadine M. Schöneck (eds), *(Un-)gerechte (Un-) Gleichheiten*, Berlin, pp. 16–26.

10 Thomas Piketty (2014), *Capital in the Twenty-First Century*, Cambridge, MA and London.

11 Joseph Vogl (2017), *The Ascendancy of Finance*, Cambridge.

12 Joseph Vogl (2015), *The Specter of Capital*, Stanford, p. 71.

13 Colin Crouch (2009), 'Privatised Keynesianism: An Unacknowledged Policy Regime', *The British Journal of Politics & International Relations* 11(3): 382–99.

14 Christian Marazzi (2012), *Sozialismus des Kapitals*, Zurich.

15 Niklas Luhmann (1971), 'Die Risiken der Wahrheit und die Perfektion der Kritik', unpublished manuscript, Bielefeld.

16 Francois Bourguignon (2015), *The Globalization of Inequality*, Princeton.

17 I am referring here to the circumplex model of James A. Russel (1980), 'A Circumplex Model of Affect', *Journal of Personality and Social Psychology* 39: 1161–78.

18 Martin Heidegger (2001 [1962]), *Being and Time*, trans. John Macquarrie and Edward Robinson, Oxford, p. 173.

19 Ibid.

20 This is the approach to the biography in developmental psychology and sociology. See e.g. Paul B. Baltes (1990), 'Entwicklungspsychologie der Lebensspanne: Theoretische Leitsätze', *Psychologische Rundschau* 41: 1–24; or Steffen Hillmert and Karl Ulrich Mayer (eds) (2004), *Geboren 1964 und 1971. Neue Untersuchungen zu Ausbildungs- und Berufschancen in Westdeutschland*, Wiesbaden.

21 Karl Jaspers (1979 [1931]), *Die geistige Situation der Zeit*, 8th edn, Berlin and New York; English trans. (2010 [1933]), *Man in the Modern Age*, London.

22 Heidegger, *Being and Time*, p. 176.

23 Heinz Bude (2015), 'Die Selbstgerechten, die Übergangenen und die Verbitterten. Die Gesellschaft der Angst und der

Protestbegriff des Volkes. Eine Dresdner Rede', *Theater heute* 3 (March): 30–5.

24 Peter Sloterdijk (2000), *Die Verachtung der Massen. Versuch über Kulturkämpfe in der modernen Gesellschaft*, Frankfurt am Main, p. 47.

25 Herbert Giersch (1985), *Eurosclerosis*, Kieler Diskussionsbeiträge 2, Kiel.

26 Mancur Olson (1985), *Aufstieg und Niedergang von Nationen*, Tübingen.

27 Claus Offe, '"Unregierbarkeit". Zur Renaissance konservativer Krisentheorien', in Jürgen Habermas (ed.) (1979), *Stichworte zur 'Geistigen Situation der Zeit'*, vol. 1, Frankfurt am Main, pp. 294–318.

28 Burkart Lutz (1984), *Der kurze Traum immerwährender Prosperität*, Frankfurt am Main/New York.

29 Steven Shapin and Simon Schaffer (1985), *Leviathan and the Air-Pump: Hobbes, Boyle and the Experimental Life*, Princeton.

30 Paul Boghossian (2006), *Fear of Knowledge: Against Relativism and Constructivism*, Oxford.

31 Nicolas Bourriaud (2002), *Relational Aesthetics*, Paris.

32 Bruno Latour (2004), *Politics of Nature: How to Bring the Sciences into Democracy*, trans. Catherine Porter, Cambridge, MA.

33 Brian Massumi (2010), *Ontopower: War, Powers and the State of Perception*, Durham, NC.

34 Timotheus Vermeulen and Robin van den Akker, 'Notes on Metamodernism', in David Rudrum (ed.) (2015), *Supplanting the Postmodern: An Anthology of Writings on the Arts and Culture of the Early 21st Century*, London, pp. 309–29, here pp. 314–15.

35 Achille Mbembe (2017), *Critique of Black Reason*, Duke University Press, p. 182.

In the Mood for 'Mood'

1 Leo Spitzer (1963), *Classical and Christian Ideas of World Harmony: Prolegomena to an Interpretation of the Word 'Stimmung'*, ed. Anna Granville Hatcher, with a foreword by René Wellek, Baltimore.

2 Ludwig Giesz (1971), *Phänomenologie des Kitsches*, Munich, pp. 55–61.
3 See David Wellbery (2003), 'Stimmung', in Karlheinz Barck et al. (eds), *Ästhetische Grundbegriffe*, vol. 5, Stuttgart and Weimar, pp. 703–33.
4 See Anna-Katharina Gisbertz (ed.) (2011), *Stimmung. Zur Wiederkehr einer ästhetischen Kategorie*, Munich; Friederike Reents and Burkhard Meyer-Sickendiek (eds) (2013), *Stimmung und Methode*, Tübingen. See also Hans Ulrich Gumbrecht (2011), *Stimmungen lesen. Über eine verdeckte Wirklichkeit der Literatur*, Munich; and Gernot Böhme (2013), *Atmosphäre. Essays zur neuen Ästhetik*, 7th edn, Berlin.
5 See e.g. Burkhard Meyer-Sickendiek and Lyrisches Gespür (2012), *Vom geheimen Sensorium moderner Poesie*, Paderborn and Munich.
6 Franco Moretti (2013), *The Bourgeois: Between History and Literature*, London and New York, p. 14.
7 Franco Moretti (2007), *Graphs, Maps, Trees: Abstract Models for Literary History*, London.
8 The famous formulation at the end of Michel Foucault (1970), *The Order of Things*, London.
9 Helmuth Plessner (1931), *Macht und menschliche Natur*, Berlin, p. 40, now in *idem* (2003), *Gesammelte Schriften in zehn Bänden*, vol. 5: *Macht und menschliche Natur*, Frankfurt am Main.
10 Sigmund Freud, 'Two Encyclopedia Articles' (1955 [1923]), in J. Strachey (trans.), *Standard Edition of the Complete Works of Sigmund Freud* (vol. 18), London, p. 253.
11 Otto Friedrich Bollnow (1941), *Das Wesen der Stimmungen* republished (2009) in *Schriften*, vol. 1, Würzburg, p. 22.
12 Heidegger, *Being and Time*, p. 176.
13 The expression of Hermann Schmitz (2014), 'Gefühle als Atmosphären', in *idem*, *Atmosphären*, Freiburg and Munich, 30–49, 31ff.
14 On this interpretation of mood by Heidegger, see Ernst Tugendhat (1979), *Selbstbewusstsein und Selbstbestimmung. Sprachanalytische Interpretationen*, Frankfurt am Main, p. 204ff.

15 Brian Parkinson, Peter Totterdell, Rob B. Briner and Shirley Reynolds (1996), *Changing Moods: The Psychology of Mood and Mood Regulation*, London, p. 8.

16 Thomas Fuchs (2013), 'Zur Phänomenologie der Stimmungen', in Friederike Reents und Burkhard Meyer-Sickendiek (eds), *Stimmung und Methode*, Tübingen, pp. 17–31, 25.

17 Lothar Schmidt-Atzert (1981), *Emotionspsychologie*, Stuttgart, p. 30ff.

18 Heinz Heckhausen (1977), 'Motivation: Kognitions-psychologische Aufspaltung eines summarischen Konstrukts', *Psychologische Rundschau* 28: 175–89, 177.

19 Wolfgang Metzger (1957), *Stimmung und Leistung*, Münster.

20 Richard S. Lazarus (1991), *Emotion and Adaptation*, New York.

21 Daniel Kahneman (2012), *Thinking, Fast and Slow*, London.

22 For an overview, see Brian Parkinson et al. (1996), *Changing Moods*.

23 Hermann Schmitz (2014), 'Atmosphärische Räume', in *idem*, 'Atmosphären', Freiburg and München, pp. 13–29, here p. 13.

24 Schmitz, 'Atmosphärische Räume', p. 19.

25 Jean-Paul Sartre (2004 [1957]), *The Transcendence of the Ego*, New York and Oxford, p. 35.

Cycles of Contagion and Spirals of Silence

1 Gabriel Tarde (1989 [1901]), *L'opinion et la foule*, Paris, online at: http://classiques.uqac.ca/classiques/tarde_gabriel/opinion_et_la_foule/tarde_opinion_et_la_foule.pdf

2 Niklas Luhmann (2009), *Die Realität der Massenmedien*, 4th edn, Wiesbaden, p. 104.

3 Gabriel Tarde, *L'opinion et la foule* (1989 [1901]), p. 10.

4 Jacques de Saint Victor (2014), *Les antipolitiques*, Paris; see ch. 1: 'La défiance n'est plus une "exception" française'.

5 Gabriel Tarde (1999 [1893]), *La Logique Social*, Paris, p. 256ff.

6 Gabriel Tarde (1912), *Penal Philosophy*, trans. Rapelje Howell, Boston, p. 323.

7 Gabriel Tarde (1989 [1901]), *L'opinion et la foule*, p. 30.

8 John Locke (1997 [1690]), *An Essay Concerning Human Understanding*, London.

9 Ibid., p. 321.

10 Gabriel Tarde (1989 [1901]), *L'opinion et la foule*, p. 47.

11 On the theoretical form and institutional anchoring of these national 'master-narratives' (Hayden White), see Richard Münch (1986), *Die Kultur der Moderne*, vol. 1, *Ihre Grundlagen und ihre Entwicklung in England und Amerika*, vol. 2: *Ihre Entwicklung in Frankreich und Deutschland*, Frankfurt am Main.

12 Lazarsfeld calls this the 'bandwagon effect'; see Paul F. Lazarsfeld, Bernard Berelson and Hazel Gaudet (1944), *The People's Choice: How the Voter Makes up his Mind in a Presidential Campaign*, New York and London , pp. 107–9.

13 Elisabeth Noelle-Neumann (1980), *Die Schweigespirale. Öffentliche Meinung – unsere soziale Haut*, Munich and Zurich.

14 Jürgen Habermas (1991), *The Structural Transformation of the Public Sphere*, trans. Thomas Burger and Frederick Lawrence, Cambridge, MA.

15 Norbert Elias (1991), *The Society of Individuals*, Oxford.

Disappointment and Engagement

1 Anselm Doering-Manteuffel and Lutz Rafael (2010), *Nach dem Boom. Perspektiven auf die Zeitgeschichte seit 1970*, 2nd edn, Göttingen.

2 Ronald Inglehart (1997), *Modernization and Postmodernization*, Princeton, NJ; Helmut Klages (2001), 'Werte und Wertewandel', in Bernhard Schäfers and Wolfgang Zapf (eds), *Handwörterbuch zur Gesellschaft Deutschlands*, 2nd edn, Opladen, pp. 726–38.

3 Helmut Fend (1996), *Sozialgeschichte des Aufwachsens. Bedingungen des Aufwachsens und Jugendgestalten im zwanzigsten Jahrhundert*, Frankfurt am Main.

4 Albert O. Hirschman (1982), *Shifting Involvements: Private Interest and Public Action*. Princeton, NJ.

5 Richard Yates (1961), *Revolutionary Road*, New York.

6 Alfred Andersch in 1958 after the publication the previous year of Enzensberger's first collection of poetry, *verteidigung der wölfe* (defence of wolves): 'At last, at last, the angry young man

has appeared amongst us.' Alfred Andersch (1958), '1 zorniger junger Mann', *Frankfurter Hefte* (February): 143–5, 143.

7 Hans Magnus Enzensberger (1979), *Einzelheiten I*, 10th edn, Frankfurt am Main, p. 171ff. (Quote trans. S. G.).

8 Inaugural speech of Federal Chancellor Willy Brandt in the Deutsche Bundestag in Bonn on 28 October 1969, www.willy. brandt.de, 2. English translation: http://germanhistorydocs. ghi-dc.org/sub_document.cfm?document_id=901

9 See Wolfgang Kraushaar (ed.) (2006), *Die RAF und der linke Terrorismus*, vol. 2. Hamburg.

10 Diedrich Diederichsen (2014), *Über Popmusik*, Cologne, p. 391.

11 Cited in Hans Ulrich Gumbrecht (2013), *After 1945: Latency as Origin of the Present*, California, p. 129.

The Relationship Between the Generations

1 According, at any rate, to Douglas Coupland (1991) in *Generation X: Tales for an Accelerated Culture*, New York.

2 Bundesagentur für Arbeit (2015), *Perspektive 2015: Fachkräfte für Deutschland*, o. O.

3 Kerstin Bund (2014), *Glück schlägt Geld. Generation Y: Was wir wirklich wollen*, Hamburg, p. 8.

4 See Christian Schmidt, Johannes Möller and Peter Windeck (2013), 'Arbeitsplatz Krankenhaus: Vier Generationen unter einem Dach', *Deutsches Ärzteblatt* 110(19): 928–33.

5 Klaus Hurrelmann and Erik Albrecht (2014), *Die heimlichen Revolutionäre. Wie die Generation Y unsere Welt verändert*, Weinheim and Basel.

6 On the use of this expression, see Thomas Gensicke in Shell Deutschland (ed.) (2010), *16. Shell Jugendstudie*, Frankfurt am Main, p. 224.

7 Hurrelmann und Albrecht, *Die heimlichen Revolutionäre*, p. 200.

8 Karl Mannheim, 'The Problem of Generations' (1972 [1927/8]), in Paul Kecskemeti (ed.), *Karl Mannheim: Essays*, London, pp. 315–16.

9 The concept of 'life technique' (Lebenstechnik) or 'existence technique' (Daseinstechnik) derives from Hans Thomae (1968),

Das Individuum und sein Welt. Eine Persönlichkeitstheorie, Göttingen, p. 329ff.

10 Heinz Bude (2017), *Society of Fear,* Cambridge, p. 70.
11 Bertram and Deuflhard, *Überforderte Generation.*
12 Wilfred R. Bion (1991), *Experience in Groups and Other Papers,* London.
13 Erik Brynjolfsson and Andrew McAfee (2014), *The Second Machine Age: Work, Progress, and Prosperity in a Time of Brilliant Technologies,* New York.
14 Karl Mannheim (1952), 'Competition as a Cultural Phenomenon', in *idem, Essays on the Sociology of Knowledge,* New York, p. 224.

The Established and the Outsiders

1 Joseph Schumpeter (1951), *Imperialism and Social Classes,* New York (German original: 'Die sozialen Klassen im ethnisch homogenen Milieu' (1953 [1927]), in *idem, Aufsätze zur Soziologie,* Tübingen, pp. 147–213.
2 Norbert Elias and John L. Scotson (1965), *The Established and the Outsiders,* London.
3 Günter Wallraff (1988), *The Lowest of the Low,* London, p. 1.
4 Well over four million copies have been sold in Germany; the book has been translated into more than thirty languages.
5 Aysel Özakin (1986), 'Ali hinter den Spiegeln', *Literatur konkret* 11: 6–9, here 6.
6 See the famous distinction made by Vilfredo Pareto (1963), *A Treatise on General Sociology,* New York, pp. 2057 and 2221. Pareto was himself referring to Machiavelli, whose use went back to the classical period.
7 Heinz Bude (2010), 'Soziale Mobilität als zentrale Herausforderung moderner Gesellschaften', in Vodafone Stiftung (ed.), *Aufstieg, Gerechtigkeit, Zusammenhalt: Zu den Herausforderungen moderner Staatlichkeit,* n.p.: pp. 56–65, 60.
8 Heinz Bude (2008), *Die Ausgeschlossenen. Das Ende vom Traum einer gerechten Gesellschaft,* Munich.
9 On the very limited advancement of East Germans into German leadership circles, see Steffen Mau (2012), *Lebenschancen. Wohin driftet die Mittelschicht?,* Berlin, p. 74ff.

The Feeling of the Sexes

1 Virginia Woolf (2001), *Three Guineas*, Oxford, p. 104.
2 Hanna Rosin (2012), *The End of Men and the Rise of Woman*, New York.
3 Christian Graf von Krockow (1998), *Die Stunde der Frauen. Bericht aus Pommern 1944 bis 1947*, 4th edn, Stuttgart.
4 Charles Perrow (1991), *Normal Accidents: Living with High-Risk Technologies*, Princeton, NJ.
5 Gunter Schmidt (2014), *Das große Der Die Das. Über die Modernisierung des Sexuellen*, 4. komplett überarbeitete und aktualisierte Neuauflage, Giessen; and Volkmar Sigusch (2013), *Sexualitäten. Eine kritische Theorie in 99 Fragmenten*, Frankfurt am Main and New York.
6 Pierre Bourdieu (2001), *Masculine Domination*, trans. Richard Nice, Stanford, p. 56.
7 Schmidt, *Der Die Das*, 12.
8 Cornelia Koppetsch and Sarah Speck (2015), *Wenn der Mann kein Ernährer mehr ist. Geschlechterkonflikte in Krisenzeiten*, Berlin, esp. p. 185ff.
9 Erving Goffman (1963), *Stigma: Notes on the Management of Spoiled Identity*, New Jersey.
10 See Volkmar Sigusch (2015), 'Ich bin in Rage angesichts unserer Sexualmoral', interview in *Magazin der Süddeutschen Zeitung* 21.
11 Koppetsch and Speck, *Wenn der Mann kein Ernährer mehr ist*, p. 206.
12 Schmidt, *Der Die Das*, p. 103ff.
13 Simon Strauss (2015), 'Sklavenhändler, hast du Arbeit für mich?', *Frankfurter Allgemeine Zeitung* (14 November), p. 15.

The Mood of the Future

1 Gilles Deleuze (1992), 'Postscript on the Societies of Control', *October* 59 (Winter): 3–7.
2 According to the former intellectual companion of Ronald Reagan, Charles Murray (2012), in *Coming Apart: The State of White America, 1960–2010*, New York.
3 Christoph Keese (2015), *Silicon Valley: Was aus dem mächtig-*

sten Tal der Welt auf uns zukommt, 5th edn, Munich. (Original in German, trans. S. G.)

4 Keese, *Silicon Valley*, p. 52. (trans. S. G.)

5 Luciano Floridi (2014), *The 4th Revolution: How the Infosphere is Reshaping Human Reality*, Oxford.

6 Ray Kurzweil (2005), *The Singularity is Near*, New York

7 Ludwig Binswanger (1956), *Drei Formen missglückten Daseins. Verstiegenheit, Verschrobenheit, Manieriertheit*, Tübingen.

8 Steven Shaviro (n.d.), *No Speed Limit: Three Essays on Accelerationism*, Minneapolis.

9 Ernst Tugendhat (2003), *Egozentrizität und Mystik. Eine anthropologische Studie*, Munich.

10 Fuchs, 'Zur Phänomenologie der Stimmungen', p. 28.

11 For Heidegger, the fundamental historical moods of gradual awakening. See Martin Heidegger (1989), *Beiträge zur Philosophie (Vom Ereignis)*, *Gesamtausgabe* vol. 65, Frankfurt am Main, p. 393ff.

12 Francisco J. Varela (1999), *Ethical Know-How: Action, Wisdom and Cognition*, Stanford.

13 Mark Greif (2004), 'A Bunch of Nobodies', *N+1*, 1.